Racism: A Very Short Introduction

VERY SHORT INTRODUCTIONS are for anyone wanting a stimulating and accessible way into a new subject. They are written by experts, and have been translated into more than 45 different languages.

The series began in 1995, and now covers a wide variety of topics in every discipline. The VSI library currently contains over 600 volumes—a Very Short Introduction to everything from Psychology and Philosophy of Science to American History and Relativity—and continues to grow in every subject area.

Very Short Introductions available now:

ABOLITIONISM Richard S. Newman
THE ABRAHAMIC RELIGIONS
  Charles L. Cohen
ACCOUNTING Christopher Nobes
ADAM SMITH Christopher J. Berry
ADOLESCENCE Peter K. Smith
ADVERTISING Winston Fletcher
AERIAL WARFARE Frank Ledwidge
AESTHETICS Bence Nanay
AFRICAN AMERICAN RELIGION
  Eddie S. Glaude Jr
AFRICAN HISTORY John Parker and
  Richard Rathbone
AFRICAN POLITICS Ian Taylor
AFRICAN RELIGIONS
  Jacob K. Olupona
AGEING Nancy A. Pachana
AGNOSTICISM Robin Le Poidevin
AGRICULTURE Paul Brassley and
  Richard Soffe
ALBERT CAMUS Oliver Gloag
ALEXANDER THE GREAT
  Hugh Bowden
ALGEBRA Peter M. Higgins
AMERICAN CULTURAL
  HISTORY Eric Avila
AMERICAN FOREIGN
  RELATIONS Andrew Preston
AMERICAN HISTORY
  Paul S. Boyer
AMERICAN IMMIGRATION
  David A. Gerber
AMERICAN LEGAL HISTORY
  G. Edward White

AMERICAN NAVAL HISTORY
  Craig L. Symonds
AMERICAN POLITICAL HISTORY
  Donald Critchlow
AMERICAN POLITICAL PARTIES
  AND ELECTIONS L. Sandy Maisel
AMERICAN POLITICS
  Richard M. Valelly
THE AMERICAN PRESIDENCY
  Charles O. Jones
THE AMERICAN
  REVOLUTION Robert J. Allison
AMERICAN SLAVERY
  Heather Andrea Williams
THE AMERICAN WEST Stephen Aron
AMERICAN WOMEN'S HISTORY
  Susan Ware
ANAESTHESIA Aidan O'Donnell
ANALYTIC PHILOSOPHY
  Michael Beaney
ANARCHISM Colin Ward
ANCIENT ASSYRIA Karen Radner
ANCIENT EGYPT Ian Shaw
ANCIENT EGYPTIAN ART AND
  ARCHITECTURE Christina Riggs
ANCIENT GREECE Paul Cartledge
THE ANCIENT NEAR EAST
  Amanda H. Podany
ANCIENT PHILOSOPHY Julia Annas
ANCIENT WARFARE
  Harry Sidebottom
ANGELS David Albert Jones
ANGLICANISM Mark Chapman
THE ANGLO-SAXON AGE John Blair

Available soon:

For more information visit our web site

www.oup.com/vsi/

Ali Rattansi

RACISM

A Very Short Introduction

SECOND EDITION

OXFORD
UNIVERSITY PRESS

OXFORD
UNIVERSITY PRESS

Great Clarendon Street, Oxford, OX2 6DP,
United Kingdom

Oxford University Press is a department of the University of Oxford.
It furthers the University's objective of excellence in research, scholarship,
and education by publishing worldwide. Oxford is a registered trade mark of
Oxford University Press in the UK and in certain other countries

First edition published in 2007
Second edition published in 2020

Impression: 1

Published in the United States of America by Oxford University Press
198 Madison Avenue, New York, NY 10016, United States of America

British Library Cataloguing in Publication Data

Data available

Library of Congress Control Number: 2019950973

ISBN 978–0–19–883479–3

Printed in Great Britain by
Ashford Colour Press Ltd, Gosport, Hampshire

For Shobhna and Parin

Acknowledgements

I am very grateful to Peter Walsh for his close reading of the text and for his excellent suggestions; they have improved the prose and have saved me from a number of errors. I have been lucky to have had such a brilliant and well-informed reader of my text.

Special thanks also to the two anonymous reviewers appointed by Oxford University Press for their very helpful comments which have also resulted in a more readable and better organized text.

I also want to thank Luciana O'Flaherty of Oxford University Press for her forensic reading of the manuscript and her very many helpful corrections and recommendations for revisions. The legal team at Oxford University Press highlighted possible problems, and I am grateful to them too for their diligence.

Shobhna's love, care, and support have been simply indispensable. My sister Parin has been a constant and terrific source of encouragement and assistance.

I could not have wished for a better editor than Jenny Nugee of Oxford University Press. Her unstinting support has been invaluable.

I am deeply grateful to them all.

Where authors are cited in the text but without titles of their publications, full details are included in the References wherever possible. For all factual statements, see the books and articles in the References for each chapter; see also the Further Reading section. Statistics come from a variety of sources, including official governmental agencies, books and articles cited in the References, and non-governmental organizations that are named wherever possible. However, note that minor changes in records, for example in employment statistics or for wealth and income distribution, occur on a continual basis, including the time taken from the writing of the text to its publication.

I accept full responsibility for any errors that remain despite rigorous checks of the factual material included in the text.

Contents

List of illustrations

Preface to the second edition

In the conclusion to the first edition of this book I argued that 'A long struggle between attempts to create post-ethnic, post-national, post-racial cosmopolitan frameworks and identities and more backward-looking projects is going to be a continuing feature of life in the 21st century.' My informed hunch has unfortunately proved to be only too correct.

This second, revised edition brings the narratives and dangers of racism up to date. In the process most of the book has been rewritten to take into account events since 2006, when I first wrote the book. I have also incorporated important developments in the analysis of racism.

Several themes from the first edition continue as threads throughout this second edition: the emphasis on the (varying) degree of ambivalence and contradiction in racist identities, and my argument for the indispensability of the concept of racialization in the analysis of racism.

Also, as will become clear in the text, I continue to believe that racism is multidimensional. Moreover, it evolves, to insinuate itself effectively in cultures of discrimination, so that simple, supposedly watertight definitions of racism, and diagnoses that pin the label 'racist' on individuals and institutions, hinder rather than help in understanding how minorities and outsiders are racialized and how institutional cultures and procedures continue to discriminate. Indeed, this is precisely where the concept of racialization becomes particularly useful.

These insights help to clarify, to take four illustrations that are discussed later, why certain types of Islamophobia might be regarded as forms of racism; why 'intersectionality' is important; how a form of 'colourblind' racism often prevails; and why a narrow definition of racism lacks the suppleness to grasp how issues such as 'national populism' and 'nativism' carry a deeper racial charge than is often understood even by those who are regarded as experts in the analysis of right-wing national populism.

I end with some significant considerations about recent developments in genomic science as well as the rise of right-wing national populism.

Developments following the decoding of the human genome have led to quite astonishing leaps in our understanding of how significant the mixing of populations has been in the past, so that inhabitants who make nativist claims within particular territories have seldom been the first or original settlers, thus comprehensively undermining these nativist narratives.

Furthermore, DNA analysis of the remains of the oldest known Briton, who lived around 10,000 years ago, known as 'Cheddar Man' because his remains were discovered in Cheddar Gorge in the south-west of England, has confirmed that early settlers in Europe had dark skins, dark enough for them to be classified in contemporary terms as 'black'. This is in keeping with the well-established finding that the first modern humans developed in Africa and then spread out across the rest of the planet.

However, this completely overturns the way in which Europeans have usually claimed that to belong to Europe individuals have to be white, as well as the notion that in the final instance, to be genuinely American too, whiteness is essential. The recovery and analysis of ancient DNA also has serious implications for claims by Hindu nationalists, for example, that the Indian Hindu population has some sort of essential, original purity. Indeed, there are no 'pure' biological populations. We are all the product of multiple migrations and mixtures. Europeans even contain some amount of Neanderthal DNA. These issues are discussed in Chapter 3.

By now millions of easily available DNA-testing kits have been sold. In a world in which migrations are on the increase, but walls and other impediments to movement are also being built, there is an understandable desire on the part of individuals to 'fix' their biological origins and their identities, and hope that DNA analysis will provide some sense of belonging. However, they may unwittingly add to the danger that biology is once again beginning to trump culture in the understanding of identity, allowing a space into which newer versions of biological, 'scientific' racism can now reinsert themselves.

Moreover, we once again find ourselves in a time, as we did a hundred years ago, when a serious understanding of 'race' and racism is urgent and may become even more important. I hope that this book contributes to the kind of clarity we need in a world in which populations are once again obsessed with seeking and defending 'purity' and 'natural', essential identities. We have been here before, except that now racial claims are increasingly being cloaked in notions like 'nativism' and the 'pure', 'authentic', or 'genuine' people.

The rise of right-wing national populism carries dangers that were last seen in the rise of Nazism and other forms of fascism which we thought would never appear again. They are discussed in Chapter 7. Of course, contemporary circumstances are different from the 1920s and 1930s, and the rise of national populism will no doubt play out differently, but there is little doubt that what seemed unimaginable just a few years ago is now coming to pass: the foundations of liberal democracies even in countries where they have been well established are experiencing an erosion of many fundamental institutional checks and balances against authoritarian rule. Racist forces have been emboldened by the rise of this right-wing authoritarianism, reflected in increased hate speech, especially in the new social media, but also in physical assaults against racialized ethnic minorities. In no other time since the defeat of the Nazis have public racist proclamations and violent racist acts been more on the move from the margins to the mainstream, in many parts of the Global North and the Global South.

This second edition is published at a timely moment in the seemingly never-ending saga of racism.

Chapter 1
'Race' and racism: some conundrums

The term *racism* was coined in the 1930s, primarily as a response to the Nazi project of making Germany *judenrein* or 'free of Jews'. The Nazis were in no doubt that Jews were a distinct race that posed a threat to the Aryan race to which authentic Germans supposedly belonged.

With hindsight it is possible to see that many of the dilemmas that have accompanied the proliferation of the notion of racism were present from the beginning. The idea that Jews were a distinct race was given currency by Nazi racial science. But before that, there was little consensus that Jews were a distinct race. Does that make it inappropriate to describe the longstanding hostility towards Jews in Christian Europe as racist? Or is it the case that racism has to be seen as a broader phenomenon that has long been part of human history? Indeed, is it part of 'human nature'—something does not necessarily require technical or scientifically accepted definitions of 'race' to be identified as racism?

After all, it can be argued that the Nazi project was only one stage in a very long history of antisemitism. And that antisemitism is one of the oldest racisms, indeed the 'longest hatred', as it has been called.

However, complications immediately arise, The term antisemitism only came into being in the late 1870s, when the German Wilhelm Marr used it to characterize his anti-Jewish movement, the Anti-Semitic League, and specifically to differentiate his project from earlier, more diffuse forms of Christian anti-Judaism, more popularly known as *Judenhass* or 'Jew hatred'. His was a self-conscious racism that required that Jews be defined as a distinct race. And 'antisemitism' had the advantage of sounding like a new, scientific concept separate from simple religious bigotry.

Thus, the key assertion of his little book was that Semitic racial (that is, biological) traits were systematically associated with the Jewish character (their culture and behaviour). Jews, according to Marr, could not help but be materialistic and scheming, and these traits meant an inevitable clash with German racial culture, which could not be anything but idealistic and generous. Marr entitled his pamphlet *The Victory of the Jews over the Germans*, because he thought that German racial characteristics meant that Germans would be unable to resist being completely overwhelmed by Jewish cunning. He blamed his own loss of a job on Jewish influence.

As we shall see, this is one particular form of 'hard' or 'classical' racism in which biology and culture are intertwined in a form in which biological features are inevitably accompanied by cultural traits in particular populations.

Was Marr justified in insisting on distinguishing his version of anti-Jewishness from other historical forms? Is racism, properly so-called, something distinct from the hostility that many would argue is a universal form of suspicion of all 'strangers' and those who have distinct cultural identities? It is after all not uncommon to hear the view that Jews have been particularly prone to victimization because of their own attempts to retain a distinct identity and their refusal to assimilate (one version of the so-called 'Jewish problem'), a type of argument that is often used against other ethnic minorities in European nation states.

The underlying logic of this sort of viewpoint is that racism is simply part of a continuum that includes, at one end, perfectly understandable and benign collective identifications that are essential for the survival of all cultural groups. At the other end, the Holocaust and other genocides are therefore to be regarded as unfortunate but inevitable episodes, varying in superficial ways but united by an essential similarity stemming from the very nature of humans as biological and cultural beings who live only in groups, are held together by common feelings of identity, and are thus impelled to maintain their collective identities.

Also, the idea of making the German nation *judenrein* seems close to the notion that has now come to be called 'ethnic cleansing'. But is all 'ethnic cleansing' racist? Or is there something distinctive about *racist* acts of hatred, expulsion, and violence? In which case, how exactly are we to distinguish between hostility based on ethnicity and that based on race? What is the difference between an ethnic group and a race? To put it somewhat differently, but making the same point, should we distinguish between *ethnocentrism* and racism?

It is clear that even the briefest inquiry into the meaning of the term racism throws up a number of perplexing questions and various cognate terms—ethnicity and ethnocentrism, nation, nationalism, and xenophobia, hostility to 'outsiders' and 'strangers', often called *heterophobia*, and so forth, which require clarification.

To complicate matters even more, it is worth remembering that historically there has been an ambiguity surrounding Jewish 'whiteness' which still persists to some degree. As we will see, the 'whiteness' of Jews, especially in the USA, as of Italians and the Irish too, has actually been gradually *achieved* in the 20th century as part of a social and political process of inclusion. As 'semites', but also as 'orientals', Jews were often regarded as not belonging to white races, while it was not uncommon in the 19th century for the English and Americans to regard the Irish as 'black' and for Italians to have an ambiguous status between white and black in the USA.

But who is to count as black? The history of US debates and legislation reveals consistent difficulties in defining the black population. A famous 'one-drop' rule was adopted in many southern states, which implied that any 'black' ancestry, however far back, consigned an individual to the wrong side of the white/ black divide, determining and (disadvantaging) where s/he could live, what kind of work was available, and whether marriage or even relationships could take place with a white partner. One drop of 'white blood', though, did not carry the same weight in assigning racial status.

The idea of racism is obviously closely tied to the concept of race, but it should be clear by now that the more one delves into the history of both notions the more puzzling they turn out to be.

Several important points emerge from considering the examples of Jews and the Irish, and some of the other groups that are discussed later. First, the idea of 'race' contains both biological and cultural elements, for example skin colour, religion, and behaviour. Second, the biological and cultural appear to combine in variable proportions in any definition of a racial group, depending upon the group and the historical period in question. And racial status, as in the 'whitening' of Jews, the Irish, and others, is subject to political negotiation and transformation.

Inevitably, therefore, the term racism has also become subject to social forces and political conflict. The idea of race was in retreat in the second half of the 20th century in the aftermath of the defeat of Nazism and discoveries in the science of genetics, although the 21st century has seen (unconvincing) attempts to revive the notion. Nowadays, there is a tendency to regard intercommunal hostilities as stemming from issues of *cultural* rather than racial difference, except on the very far right and among some who (misleadingly) base their assertions on recent biomedical research.

Many commentators argue that the justification of hostility and discrimination on grounds of culture rather than race is mostly a rhetorical ploy to get around the taboo against racism that has gradually been established, especially in Western liberal democracies. There is, they contend, a new 'cultural racism' that has increasingly supplanted an older biological racism. 'Islamophobia' has been identified as one of the most recent forms of this new racism. But can a combination of religious and other cultural antipathy be described as racist? Is this not to rob the idea of racism of any analytical specificity and open the floodgates to a conceptual inflation that simply undermines the legitimacy of the idea? These issues are discussed later in the book.

Fewer and fewer people in Western societies will nowadays openly describe themselves as racist. Yet social scientists, politicians, journalists, and members of various communities are apt to claim that these societies are deeply racist. Government agencies continue to collect statistical and other evidence of racial discrimination and use a variety of laws and other instruments to attempt to enforce non-discriminatory codes of conduct.

In Britain considerable controversy was ignited in 1999 when the inquiry by Sir William Macpherson into the murder of the black teenager Stephen Lawrence concluded that the London Metropolitan Police was *institutionally racist*, thus propelling yet another definition into the public domain.

This has been only one in a whole series of other investigations that have documented systematic and longstanding discrimination against Britain's ethnic minorities in spheres such as housing, private and public sector employment, and so forth.

To take instances from studies on UK medical staff, on 5 September 2018 the UK *Guardian* newspaper published findings from research that white senior doctors earned almost £5,000 more than colleagues from minority ethnic backgrounds. A 2014 study, titled *The Snowy White Peaks of the NHS*, carried out by the Middlesex University Business School, exposed the absence of British minority ethnic (BME) representation in higher-level posts in the National Health Service (NHS), while a national review by the NHS in 2016 reported that much higher proportions of BME medical staff reported cases of harassment, bullying, and abuse. This follows a Bradford University study, which surveyed eighty NHS trusts between June 2008 and November 2009 and found that BME staff were nearly twice as likely to face disciplinary procedures than their white counterparts (see the BBC News article titled '"Institutional racism is an issue" in NHS, says ex-executive', 7 November 2012, although the Department of Health is reported to have said that the NHS was not institutionally racist). Research by the King's Fund and what is now known as the Race Equality Foundation, and other related organizations, has revealed that black and Asian British citizens receive worse treatment compared with whites as patients of the NHS, and that this is especially true in the case of mental health services.

Although these findings and events have been greeted with disbelief in some quarters, to many this came as no surprise. As reported in the *British Medical Journal* (*BMJ*) on 5 March 1988, a Commission for Racial Equality investigation had already revealed that London's highly respected St George's Hospital Medical School's admission procedures had unwittingly inscribed into the school's computer software a systematic penalty against British applicants with non-European-sounding surnames, as well as against females. The report in the *BMJ* points out that the computer program had incorporated 'a bias that was already in the system', that is, such discriminatory practices on the grounds of ethnic origin and sex had been normally implemented by staff before the computer program was written in an attempt to simplify and speed up admissions procedures. The *BMJ* rightly argues that such attitudes 'cannot be excused'. The process has been revised to give all applicants a fair chance.

The issue of the exclusion of ethnic minorities from top-ranking universities in the UK, especially Oxford and Cambridge, has assumed prominence in debates about racial inequality in the period since 2010. Moreover, on 6 July 2019 the *Guardian* newspaper published findings from its freedom of information requests to 131 British universities, revealing that in the previous five years at least 996 formal complaints regarding racism had been made by staff and students. A total of 367 were upheld, resulting in at least seventy-eight student suspensions or exclusions, and fifty-one suspensions, dismissals, and resignations by staff. The authors of the *Guardian* article, David Batty and Sally Weale, claim that there were grounds to believe that these figures underestimate the scale of racism in universities because many students and staff were dissuaded from making complaints, or were persuaded to drop them or agreed to a more informal resolution.

In the USA, the pervasive white domination of Oscar nominations in the film industry has aroused controversy as another indication of issues around racism. Both Oxbridge and the USA have experienced movements to knock down statues: in the former, of the racist colonialist Cecil Rhodes; and in the latter, those of Confederate generals who wanted to uphold slavery as an ongoing institution.

In March 2017, the UK government published a 'Race Disparity Audit' which, among other things, showed that the rate of 'stop and search' by police in 2016–17 among black people was 29 for every 1,000, while that for whites was 4 per 1,000. On the other hand, from 2007–8 to 2015–16, the percentage of black and other ethnic minority students among the total students in British universities increased from 17.2 per cent to 22.9 per cent, while for white students the figure fell from 82.8 per cent to 77.1 per cent. However, these gross figures hide the wide disparity between the entry of ethnic minorities and white entry into the top universities in the UK, as well as the class and gender disparities within both groups, thus requiring a more differentiated examination of these gross statistics: they hide as much as they reveal. What role *racism* plays in the variety of disparities in policing and education is a complex matter.

Note that in Germany revulsion against the Nazi past has meant that 'xenophobia' (*Ausländerfeindlichkeit*) rather than racism is the preferred term in German public discourse, raising yet more questions. Obviously, the relationship between xenophobia and racism requires clarification, especially as the issue of immigration has animated the rise of far-right parties all over Europe.

In the USA, of course, there are continuing examples of controversy over 'race' and racism, over and above the question of statues of Confederate generals. The election of President Trump in November 2016 was, in part, attributed by his opponents to his so-called 'dog-whistle racism' against ethnic minorities and immigrants, especially of Mexican and Muslim origin. In July 2019 President Trump's tweets arguing that four Democratic congresswomen of colour—three of whom had been born in the USA and one who had arrived as a child refugee—'should go back home' was condemned by the Democrat-controlled House of Representatives as 'racist'.

Over two decades ago, two criminal trials revealed an American population strongly divided on 'black/white' lines. Prior to his trial and consideration of the evidence by the jury, O. J. Simpson, a well-known sportsman, was believed by most white people to be guilty and most African Americans not guilty of the murder of his white wife. He was acquitted. The acquittal in a state court of four white police officers seen on camera beating a black motorist, Rodney King, led to widespread 'race' rioting in Los Angeles in 1992. A federal trial led to the conviction of two of the officers.

The more recent death of black American citizens—such as Eric Garner on 17 July 2014—at the hands of police officers in the second decade of the 21st century has sparked widespread revulsion, and has now given rise to considerable anger and the development of the Black Lives Matter movement, although it is worth noting that African Americans are much more likely to attribute the killings to racism than white Americans.

The Black Lives Matter movement has also been involved in publicizing the fact that one in nine African American males between the ages of twenty and thirty-four are in prison, and indeed are more likely to be incarcerated than to be attending college. The US Department of Justice confirmed in 2014 that the majority of male prisoners between the ages of thirty and thirty-nine are black, with Hispanics making up 2 per cent and whites 1 per cent. The likelihood of a black man spending time in prison at some point in his life is one in three, while for Hispanic men it is one in six and for white men it is one in seventeen. One consequence is that African Americans are disproportionately disenfranchised, as many states in the USA are especially punitive in denying voting rights to those convicted of felonies. Moreover, as reported by the American Death Penalty Information Center, defendants convicted of killing whites are considerably more likely to be sentenced to death than defendants convicted of killing blacks. The centre also reports studies which show that the odds of receiving a death sentence are nearly four times higher if the defendant is black.

In one form or another, then, the issue of 'race' is very much alive, not only in the UK and the USA, but also western and eastern Europe, as we shall see.

Chapter 2
Imperialism, genocide, and the 'science' of race

The term 'race' entered English early in the 16th century. This was also the time when the term was acquiring currency in other European languages, for example *'rassa'* and *'race'* in French, *'razza'* in Italian, *'raca'* in Portuguese, and *'raza'* in Spanish. By the middle of the 16th century one common meaning was beginning to gain ground. Race began to refer to family, lineage, and breed. The term had particularly come to signify continuity over generations in aristocratic and royal families.

The concept of race that we have inherited is also a modern idea, with different origins, but whose meaning was bolted on to this early usage. It was primarily born out of the encounters of white European travellers with darker-skinned peoples outside Europe from the 15th century onwards.

1492

When Columbus set out on his momentous journey to what he thought was Asia, the significance of the year, 1492, was not lost on him, for this was the year that both Muslims and Jews were expelled from Spain. He wrote at the head of the first journal of his travels: 'In this present year 1492, after your Highnesses have brought to an end the war against the Moors...in this very month...your Highnesses...determined to send me...to the said regions of India…Thus after having driven all the Jews out of your realms and dominions, Your Highnesses…commanded me to set out with a sufficient Armada to…India.'

The year that is often regarded as marking the birth of Western modernity was one symbolized by the expulsion of internal 'others' and the beginning of the conquest and pillage of those beyond the Christian, 'civilized' world. The significance of the fact that the modern era can be said to begin with forms of 'racial' aggression should not be lost on us. The modernity inaugurated by the voyages has yet to escape fully the shadows cast by the conquests of Spain and the Americas.

The 'Indians' discover Columbus

The shores on which Columbus landed, as we now know, were far from the 'Indies'. But he was convinced that he had found what he was looking for.

The Caribs and Arawaks who occupied the islands Columbus chanced upon were sophisticated peoples. They were familiar with agriculture, could make pottery of various designs, and were skilled mariners.

Columbus, though, saw a primitive people, unclothed and dark, and therefore close to nature and uncivilized. And he had come looking for gold and to spread the word of the Christian God.

Race, nature, and gender: the ambiguous legacy of the Enlightenment

It was in the 18th-century period of great intellectual fervour and social change, generally referred to as the Enlightenment, that the idea of race began to be incorporated into more systematic meditations on the nature of the world. Europe made a decisive transition to a distinctly modern age, beyond Columbus's Christianity, with the Enlightenment.

The Enlightenment is usually dubbed the Age of Reason. It is regarded as one which enthroned rationality as the highest human capacity. But the emphasis on reason was counterbalanced by an appreciation of pleasure, passion, and the role of emotions.

The period was also characterized, on the part of some of its leading figures, by veneration for the wisdom and civilization of the Orient. China, especially, was admired for its wisdom, technical achievements, and civilization. *Chinoiserie* and *Sinophilia* were notable features of the mid-18th century in France. It became fashionable to have Chinese gardens, porcelain, and even mock Chinese villages.

Racial classification and the Enlightenment

The form of rationality that predominated in the Enlightenment was primarily classificatory, and the manner in which the idea of race was increasingly pressed into service to make sense of natural variety reflected this classificatory zeal. The central issue that framed the various classificatory schemes was whether all humans were one species.

The most influential of the classificatory systems of the 18th century was produced by the Swedish naturalist Carl Linnaeus. In the volumes of his *Systema Naturae*, published from 1735 onwards, *Homo sapiens* was united by the ability to mate with all humans, and Linnaeus proposed a fourfold classification of humans: *americanus* (red, choleric, and erect), *europaeus* (white and muscular), *asiaticus* (yellow, melancholic, and inflexible), and *afer* (black, phlegmatic, and indulgent). Linnaeus's attempt to find connections between appearance and temperament can also be gauged from the following passages from the 1792 English edition: '*H. Europaei*. Of fair complexion, sanguine temperament,

1. Troglodyte and Pygmy: examples of Linnaean types. The classification has clear evaluative judgements built into it.

and brawny form...Of gentle manners, acute in judgement, of quick invention, and governed by fixed laws...*H. Afri*. Of black complexion, phlegmatic temperament, and relaxed fibre...Of crafty, indolent, and careless disposition, and are governed in their actions by caprice' (see Figure 1).

Blackness, sexuality, and aesthetics

The two greatest philosophers of the 18th century, Kant (now regarded by some as the first proper theorist of race) and Hume, were equally prone to evaluating the moral and intellectual worth of different peoples classified, especially, by skin colour. Kant proclaimed in 1764: 'This fellow was quite black...a clear proof that what he said was stupid.'

Kant drew explicitly on the revised version of David Hume's *On National Characters* (1754) where the Scottish philosopher confidently announced:

I am apt to suspect the negroes in general and all species of men
(for there are four or five different kinds) to be naturally inferior to
the whites. There never was a civilized nation of any other
complexion than white...No ingenious manufactures amongst
them, no arts, no sciences. On the other hand, the most rude and
barbarous of the whites, such as the ancient Germans, the present
Tartars have still something eminent about them.

Kant and Hume's acquaintance with black people was negligible.
But from early in the 16th century, Portuguese, Spanish, and
English adventurers had started bringing West Africans to
Europe.

It soon became fashionable to have black servants at court and in
aristocratic households, dressed in the finest clothes to display the
wealth of the masters. But by the 1590s the black presence had
become a pawn in domestic politics. During a period of famine
and economic recession, Elizabeth I, having had a number of
black servants, attempted to expel all black people.

Elizabeth's attempted expulsion of blacks was singularly
unsuccessful. By the middle of the 18th century there were
perhaps some 20,000 black people living in Scotland and
England. By the end of the 18th century several black writers had
published books. One of them, Ignatius Sancho, was friendly with
a number of prominent literary figures, including Samuel
Johnson.

Nevertheless, the dominant image of the black was that of
brutishness and bestiality. There was, especially, an association
between blackness and ugliness, and between beauty and moral
virtue. Aesthetics in the 17th and 18th centuries was dominated by
the assumption that the ideal form of all human beauty could be
found in Greek and Roman art. The most influential historian of
art in the 18th century, Johann Joachim Winckelmann, devised a

scale of beauty that highlighted certain features of antique sculptures as the embodiment of beauty. Winckelmann regarded the depressed nose as particularly ugly. The African could not but fall foul of this European ideal of beauty and moral worth (see Figure 2).

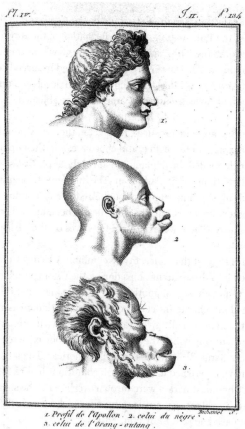

Pl. IV.   *T. II.*   *P. 134.*

1. Profil de l'Apollon. 2. celui du nègre.
3. celui de l'Orang-outang.

Duhamel S.

2. A classical Greek profile juxtaposed with those of 'Negro' and ape, purporting to show the similarity between the 'facial angles' of the 'Negro' and the ape.

The question of slavery

There is little doubt that doctrines of race gained considerable strength with the growth of the slave trade. The idea of African racial inferiority was intrinsic to justifications for their enslavement.

British involvement in the slave trade began to take off in the middle of the 17th century, with the formation of the Royal African Company. This trade reinforced the view that the African was subhuman. African slavery was legitimized by already existing views of Africans as inferior, which were then developed once the institution of African slavery became firmly established.

The growing appetite for sugar, to sweeten the newly popular but bitter beverages of tea, coffee, and chocolate, and the popularity of rum punch, fuelled the demand for slave labour on British-owned sugar plantations in the Caribbean. The infamous triangular trade involved ships sailing from Liverpool, Bristol, and London carrying textiles, guns, cutlery, glass, beads, beer, and other British manufactures. These were bartered for slaves on the African coast.

Estimates suggest that at least twelve million Africans were crammed into these sailing ships during the whole period of slavery, although at least another four million may have died in the forced marches to the slave ports and the 'Middle Passage'. This is the name usually given to the extraordinarily inhumane conditions during which the slaves were transported across the Atlantic to Jamaica, Barbados, and the Americas. The large numbers who perished in these harsh conditions before they reached their destination were thrown overboard. The survivors were exchanged for sugar, rum, tobacco, and spices which were brought back and sold in Britain.

Slavery generated huge amounts of wealth for British traders and planters, and was crucial to the growth of Bristol, Liverpool, and

Glasgow. Huge fortunes were amassed by slave traders and planters and played a significant part in ensuring that Britain became the world's pre-eminent industrial economy and banking centre, and the dominant political and military power.

Slave traders and plantation owners had a crucial interest in representing blacks as fit for no other fate. And they claimed a special knowledge of blacks. Edward Long, the son of a Jamaican planter, was typical. Long believed that blacks were a separate species. Unsurprisingly, he drew the conclusion that slavery civilized the African.

The 'science' of race

In the 19th century there emerged a whole range of theories that explained all human variation on the basis of innate racial characteristics. The theories of Robert Knox, published in *The Races of Men* (1850), and the Frenchman Count Arthur de Gobineau, who published his *Essay on the Inequality of Human Races* in 1854, may be taken as typical examples. Such views were united by a variety of assumptions.

First, that humankind could be divided into a limited number of distinct and permanent races, and that race was the key concept for an understanding of human variation. Second, that there were distinct physical markers that characterized the different races, especially skin colour, facial features, texture of hair, and, with the growing influence of phrenology, size and shape of skull. Third, that each race was innately associated with distinct social, cultural, and moral traits. Fourth, that the races could be graded in a coherent hierarchy of talent and beauty, with whites at the top and blacks at the bottom.

A consideration of Gobineau's views highlights other important themes in scientific racism. Gobineau regarded history as the history of a struggle between different races—white, yellow, and black—but conflates *race* with *class*, so that the history of every 'social order' is the result of conquest by a dominant race, which then forms the nobility, a bourgeois class that is of mixed origins, and a lower class, 'the common people'.

Robert Knox (1791–1862) wanted to convince his contemporaries that the main political conflicts in Europe had an underlying racial basis. He distinguished between Scandinavians, who were supposedly innately democratic, but were incapable of extending democracy to the peoples they subjugated; Celts, who were good fighters but with little political virtue; Slavonians, who had potential but lacked leadership; and the Sarmatians or Russ, who were incapable of real progress in science or literature. True to the principles of the racial theories of the day, though, Knox regarded the darker races as being furthest away from the fair Saxons, and posited that the greatest degree of natural animosity would prevail between these darker and fairer races.

For the present, two other features of this phase of scientific racism should be noticed. First, many of those involved in trying to prove the inferiority of black and yellow populations were also trying to find scientific justification for the inferiority of women. With the growing popularity of the measurement of skull and brain size, it was often claimed that women's low brain weight and deficient brain structures were similar to those of the lower races, and this explained their supposedly inferior intellectual abilities. Moreover, women and the lower races were regarded as being impulsive, emotional, and unable to engage in the abstract reasoning that was the preserve of the white male.

Science and pathology

A related phenomenon was the medicalization of racial analysis, again with strong overtones of sexuality. The two elements combined in the study of black women and prostitutes.

The 19th century's scientific racism sought external signs of the black woman's excessive, animal-like sexuality in the supposedly distinctive appearance of her sexual organs. In 1815 an autopsy was performed on a Saartje Baartman, also known as Sarah Baartman, and more popularly as the Hottentot Venus, to reveal more clearly her buttocks and her genitalia. Before her death she had been exhibited to European audiences so that they could gape at her steatopygia, or protruding buttocks.

Medical discourses began to relate studies of the physiology and physiognomy of white prostitutes to analyses of black female bodies to create a powerful chain of association connecting blackness and women's innately pathological sexuality.

Race and nation

The idea of nation has had a crucial role in the origins and development of racial thinking. A contrast between *race* and *nation* was famously made by Johann Gottfried Herder (1744–1803). Herder argued that nations were made up of many races. Over long periods of time each nation had developed a unique culture and civilization, a *Volksgeist*, expressed especially in its language, myths, and songs—a whole way of living that was incommensurate with the cultures of other nations, all of them unique. There was a short distance between notions of *Volksgeist* and racial character.

After the 1789 revolution, the French nation was seen as united by being a voluntary association of free and equal citizens. The French enjoyed membership of the community by virtue of their residence in national territory, irrespective of ethnic origin and religion.

But the universalism of the civic models of nationhood was also easily compromised by the particularism of race. In France, national republicans in the 1840s often drew upon the idea of invading Germans oppressing native Gauls. Antisemitism, too, remained a potent force.

Whiteness, blackness, and the promiscuity of 'race'

Above all, the idea of the nation enabled a new boundary between 'them' and 'us' based upon a mixture of people, culture, and race.

This process was facilitated by the fact that no two scientists of race could agree on a classification of races. Skin colours obstinately shaded into each other. Combined with the vagueness of the findings of phrenology and physiognomy, both of which eventually collapsed, a wide range of races were being invented according to the whims of individual racial theorists. Myriad cultural and political traits such as democracy and authoritarianism were arbitrarily attached to races.

Territorial and national concepts—'Prussians', for example—could not be kept strictly separate from racial notions of Teutons and Saxons, or Nordic types. Similar problems were encountered in defining the English, French, or Italian nations.

Elements of social class and sexual difference could also be incorporated. Lower classes and women, just as much as different nations and races, could be denied full membership of the nation because of their supposedly inferior capacity for rationality and self-government when compared to the white, propertied male.

Historically it did not take long for ideas of nation, race, 'people', citizenship, and popular sovereignty to coalesce. The formation of strong states had a crucial role in this process. As the European nation states developed a more definite cultural uniformity, so the division between a nation's citizens and foreigners hardened. It was increasingly held that distinctively French, German, and Italian national characteristics had been nurtured by long, shared histories. Thus, non-nationals could be defined as potential invaders or traitors.

The outsider became a potential carrier of pollution who could infect the body politic. Conceptions of 'motherland' and 'fatherland' explicitly encouraged associations of biological kinship between citizens of the nation state.

In the racial theories of Gobineau, issues of class and sexuality, always open to incorporation, as we have seen, became intertwined with those of nation and race. Fears about the racial origins and characteristics of the lower classes had been important in post-Enlightenment Europe. Projects of nation formation had involved the cultural transformation of peasantries and the rapidly growing urban populations of the poor and industrial workers into good French or Italian nationals. And conceptions of proper masculinity and femininity, the idea of authentic German or French men and women, were intrinsic to the idea of national character and health.

Not surprisingly, the immigrant poor came to be seen as a particular problem. In Britain, the arrival of the Irish, fleeing famine and living in appalling conditions in the cities, provoked virulent hostility. There was a widely held view that the Irish were ape-like.

'Internal' racisms in Europe

Ideas of race derived nourishment as much from concerns internal to Europe as from the growing encounters with non-Europeans in the period of early modernity. Schemes of classification of human variety that mushroomed in the 18th and 19th centuries were as anxious about drawing boundaries between white European races or 'nations'—Gauls, Saxons, Slavs, and others—as between whites, blacks, and Orientals.

Growing nationalisms and a conservative reaction to the collapsing hierarchies of the aristocratic order combined to create fertile breeding grounds for what have sometimes been called 'internal racisms'. In particular, as industrialization began to take off there were increasing anxieties about the need to control the burgeoning landless labourers flooding into the fast-growing cities. Imperial expansion provided essential intellectual and economic resources in a new social landscape in which class was racialized, and race became intertwined with class and gender in the government of colonial populations.

Race, class, gender, and empire

The growing industrial working class began to be seen as a 'breed' and 'race' apart from the middle and upper classes. At the same time the urban slums in which they were compelled to live were described in the language of imperialism, as foreign lands full of 'swamps' and 'wilderness', requiring similar degrees of policing and social control over their degenerate habits.

Moreover, concepts of racial abnormality were superimposed on ideas of sexual and other types of social deviance. Militant sections of the working class, the Irish, Jews, homosexuals, prostitutes, and the insane were regarded as racial deviants. Women who worked and thus transgressed the Victorian boundary between private and public were treated as examples of racial regression.

Metaphors of the family, paternalism, and historical progress allowed women, the working class, and inferior races in the colonies to be portrayed as childlike, requiring the firm but benign hand of white middle- and upper-class males. The empire was thus seen as a 'family', with both women and inferior races being part of a natural order ruled over by privileged white males at home and abroad.

This went hand in hand with what one might call the effeminization of the natives in the colonies. Colonized lands were given feminine names, Virginia being the most obviously sexualized.

In British imperial projects the effeminization of colonial subjects combined with a class-divided reconstruction of British masculinities. Conceptions of upper-class masculinity, especially of those entrusted with running the empire, institutionalized in the exclusive 'public' schools, emphasized sexual self-restraint and lack of emotional display.

At the same time, the masculinism of imperialism enabled a construction of the middle-class English woman as chaste, frail, and in need of protection, but also precious as the progenitor of an imperial race. This made her a useful pawn in a narrative that included sexually predatory colonial natives and working-class Englishmen, as well as the sexually available and erotic 'native' woman, a staple of sexual fantasies fed by narratives published by colonial administrators and the growing number of travellers.

The sexual attraction of the Oriental woman, especially, introduced a complication in colonial rule that further destabilized the logic of a simple racial inferiorization of dark-skinned races. As the historian William Dalrymple has shown, in the early stages of British expansion in India, in the 18th century, it was common for British men to adopt Indian modes of dress, to live in dwellings with Indian furnishings, to offer prayers to Indian deities, and to fall in love with and marry Indian women. Homosexuals too found the Orient a more congenial and permissive place.

However, more distant, brutal forms of domination took shape in the 19th century. The 1857 Indian Mutiny and the 1865 rebellion in Jamaica were particularly influential in inaugurating a more repressive mode of rule in the colonies.

The case of colonial culture as it developed in India is instructive in exhibiting imperial racism in all its complexity. Conceptions of 'Hindoos' as an inferior race, and Indian society as despotic and stagnant, coexisted with admiration for both Muslim and Hindu architecture and for achievements in arts and industry, especially the manufacture of textiles. The sexual allure of the Indian woman became an important motif of travel lore. Indian intellectual abilities were highly regarded, leading to the famous proposal by Macaulay in 1835 of an education system for producing 'a class of persons, Indian in blood and colour, but English in taste, opinions, in morals, and in intellect' who would act as 'interpreters between us and the millions whom we govern'.

This led to the setting up of English-language schools and universities throughout India, beginning a process of Anglicization that fed into a nationalist movement that was eventually to lead to the overthrow of British rule.

The study of India's ancient language, Sanskrit, by various scholars, but especially William Jones (1746–94), who founded the Asiatick Society of Bengal, led to the translation of key ancient texts such as the Hindu epic *Bhagavad Gita*, and opened up to the European gaze the sophistication of Indian mythology, metaphysics, and religion.

The impact of these Indian texts was even more powerful in Germany, where Romantic intellectuals drew upon Indian sources to nurture their reaction against what they regarded as the excessive rationalism of the Enlightenment. The German Idealist movement of which Herder, Goethe, Schelling, and Schopenhauer were leading lights were particularly attracted by what they regarded as the parallel philosophical idealism of India, especially the belief that in the final analysis all things form a single whole, and that this oneness arises from the fundamentally spiritual nature of reality. Many European scholars believed that all religion and civilization had Indian origins. As Friedrich Schlegel

(1772–1829) wrote, 'Everything, yes, everything has its origins in India'. The veneration was accompanied, however, by doses of primitivism. Indians were seen as childlike in their innocence and gentle behaviour, and feminine in their supposed deviousness and cowardliness. As becomes clear from Ashis Nandy's brilliant exploration in *Intimate Enemy* (1983), there was no single stereotype, only contradictory ones that characterized European imperial discourses on Indians.

Orientalism and race

Influenced by the insights of the French social philosopher Michel Foucault (1927–84) into the intertwining of knowledge, power, and rule, especially as deployed in the Arab American cultural critic Edward Said's *Orientalism* (1978) and the new field of 'postcolonialist studies', modern scholars are much more aware of the way colonial knowledges were directly and indirectly implicated in subjugating colonized populations in imperialist projects. Thus, it is now much better understood how the interest shown in Indian culture by the early Orientalists fed directly into notions and practices by which India was governed and Indian culture shaped according to Orientalist preoccupations. Sanskrit was learned not just to better understand Indian culture in its own right, but also to allow a better grafting of colonial administration onto indigenous customary laws.

The nature of the Indian population was documented in myriad surveys and censuses. Most significant in the present context is the British colonial authority's attempted *racial* classification of the Indian population.

The division of India into two main races, in particular, became established as a basis for army recruitment. India was said to be divided between a fair-complexioned, Sanskrit-speaking, martial people of 'Aryan' descent who had made their way from the north-west, and a darker-skinned, more inferior race. The 'Aryans' were regarded as a people with European origins, especially because of the notion of a common group of Indo-Aryan and European languages. Of course, this posed a potential problem about the possible equality of the European colonizers and the Indo-Aryans, an anomaly that was resolved by the suggestion that the original Aryans had suffered racial degeneration by mixing with the dark-skinned Dravidian and other races. Thus India was linked to Europe's past only in antiquity.

In framing rules for a more direct rule over India after the shock of the 1857 rebellion, British administrators compiled handbooks advising that the more 'martial races' of the Punjab, and subsequently those of Gurkha origin, were the most suitable for recruitment into the army, both on grounds of martial prowess and loyalty to British rule.

Racial typologies of Indians became intertwined with caste divisions. Whereas caste had been one of many social divisions around which the traditional social life of Indians had been organized, together with temple, clan, village, linguistic, and regional identities, overlain with divisions of trade and occupation, the British insisted on a simplified four-caste differentiation and emphasized caste as the most central organizing principle of Indian culture. Furthermore, only members of the Brahman caste were regarded as being of proper Aryan stock.

The most recent genetic research, based on the analysis of ancient bone DNA, as discussed by David Reich, has painted a more complex picture of social divisions in ancient India, as we shall see in Chapter 3.

Eugenics, social Darwinism, and imperial racism

The late Victorian era saw a significant cultural realignment; from a period in which gender, race, nation, and class had been closely intertwined, emerged a phase in which race assumed greater importance.

Several factors were responsible. First, there was the coincidence between the Morant Bay black rebellion in Jamaica in 1865 (coming relatively soon after the Indian rebellion of 1857) and the growing momentum of the reform movement for extending suffrage to much larger sections of the working class. This political mobilization culminated in the 1867 Reform Act which enfranchised employed, married, male householders in Britain.

The result was a more rigid line between whites, deserving of the vote, and the blacks and other natives who—depending on the point of view—were either not ready for enfranchisement or were inherently inferior, could never govern themselves, and were only fit to serve white interests in the British Empire.

Second, the idea of empire became part of a widespread popular culture of racism. As trade within the empire grew by leaps and bounds, so advertising, in particular, disseminated even more widely images of blacks as uncivilized and inferior, but smiling, happy, and grateful in their subservience. The empire was charged with 'the white man's burden' of bringing Christianity, and especially hygiene, to 'coloured' peoples. Particularly striking were the ubiquitous soap advertisements, which equated being 'coloured' with being dirty, a condition which could be metaphorically and literally cleansed away and whitened by the regular use of soap (see Figure 3).

Third, the very success of the European, but especially British, imperial project gave widespread legitimacy to the obviousness of white racial superiority, thus including social classes in a joint venture. By 1914, the European powers held 85 per cent of the globe as possessions of one kind or another.

3. *Gossages' Magical Soap,* **blackness equated with dirt.**

Finally, social Darwinism and the eugenics movement reinforced the belief in race as the key human division.

Eugenics

Charles Darwin held that all humans belonged to the same species. In principle, his book *The Origin of Species* (1859), and even more so *The Descent of Man* (1871), were not reconcilable with the scientific racism of the age. The notion of race rested on the supposition of the characteristics of races remaining stable over time. Darwin's theory of evolution by natural selection privileged change, based on the role of random variations within populations in producing adaptation to changing circumstances.

But his ideas were soon absorbed into prevailing ideas of scientific racism, especially by the group that has come to be called 'social Darwinists'. Chief among the social Darwinists was the English sociologist Herbert Spencer (1820–93). It was Spencer who coined the famous phrase 'survival of the fittest', which sanctioned the belief that the technological advances and refined customs of the white races were proof of their greater 'fitness' and the natural necessity that they rule over darker, inferior races.

Social Darwinism nurtured eugenics, a stream of racial thinking that dominated the period from the 1880s to the 1930s in both the USA and Europe. A key figure was Francis Galton, cousin of Charles Darwin. A sense of his views is evident in his belief that English settlers to the USA, Canada, and Australia had in effect led to the self-banishment of racially inferior whites, leaving behind 'a better class of Englishmen'.

Galton became especially interested in mapping differing degrees of intelligence among human populations. But Galton had no clear means of understanding and assessing intelligence. It is hardly surprising that his 1869 *Hereditary Genius* concluded, on the basis of completely unsystematic observation, that the highest levels of intelligence among dogs was greater than that among the lowest Australian Aborigines, Negroes, Englishmen, and ancient Greeks. Galton and the eugenicists also proposed the doctrine of 'intellectual dysgenesis', which claimed to chart a process of intellectual degeneration in which less intelligent classes reproduced at a higher rate than more intelligent ones. Left unchecked, the result would be an overall dilution of intelligence and a collapse of social institutions.

Two sets of events gave particular impetus to the growth of the movement. First, there was shock in Britain when the poor physical condition of recruits for the Boer War came to light. Second, in the USA, the rapid rise in immigrant numbers of 'non-Teutonic' and non-'Anglo-Saxon' whites—the Irish, Italians,

Poles, Serbs, and Greeks—and then the Chinese, heightened fears that the superior Anglo-Saxons were being swamped by inferior beings with high birth rates.

In 1894 the Immigration Restriction League (IRL) was founded. By 1924 the IRL had succeeded in convincing Congress of the dangers of racial degeneration. The Immigration Act of that year favoured immigration from 'Nordic' countries. The restrictions thus imposed were only finally dismantled by the Cellar Act of 1965, which regulated immigration solely by order of application.

The Nazi eugenics movement for 'race hygiene' (*Rassenhygiene*) was not uniformly antisemitic. Indeed, between 1904 and 1918 the race hygiene movement contained many Jewish members who supported the programme of improving German genetic stock through selective breeding. However, it was soon pressed into supporting the virulently antisemitic Nazi project.

Recent years have seen an extraordinary resurgence of research on the Holocaust (a term that only came into widespread use in the 1960s). We now know more than we have ever done about the minutiae of unfolding events as Hitler's regime hurtled towards the 'Final Solution', the physical extermination of all Jews within their grasp.

The lessons of the Holocaust

The idea that the Holocaust was an irrational, barbaric, evil aberration—a collective national psychosis that briefly interrupted the march of a tolerant, liberal, democratic German culture which has otherwise embodied some of the highest ideals of Western civilization—is no longer tenable, although some of the antisemitic propaganda of the Nazis was very crude (see Figure 4).

Hannah Arendt, the influential German Jewish intellectual who reported in the mid-1960s on the trial of Adolf Eichmann in

4. Nazi propaganda caricaturing the Jew and exaggerating the supposedly Aryan features of the German.

Jerusalem after his capture by Israeli secret agents, used the fateful phrase 'the banality of evil', in an attempt to suggest that an unprepossessing and dull bureaucrat, once he had been placed in the situation of a distant executioner, could commit quite horrific crimes. It gave rise to a sentiment that, given appropriate circumstances and powers, anyone was capable of carrying out genocidal acts.

Zygmunt Bauman, the Jewish sociologist of Polish origin, argued much the same in his frequently discussed *Modernity and the Holocaust* (1989), placing particular emphasis on the dehumanizing and distancing effects of normal bureaucratic procedures which in turn allowed a dehumanization of humans as quantities of cargo to be transported and disposed of. However, as

I showed in my 2017 book on Bauman, both Arendt and Bauman failed to note that Eichmann was a rabid antisemite, and that Hitler's single-minded obsession with expelling and then killing Jews played a key role in the Holocaust. In other words, and among other things, it is highly questionable to underplay the role of a racist ideology of antisemitism in the genocide against the Jews.

While a detailed exploration of the causes of the Holocaust is beyond the scope of this book, some important conclusions can be drawn from the considerable body of research on the subject.

First, without Hitler's single-minded pursuit of making Germany *judenrein*, the Holocaust would not have taken place. Individuals are not peripheral to major racist genocides. Second, antisemitism was only one of a number of factors, including the perilous state of the German economy, that contributed to the rise of Hitler. Third, an event like the Holocaust does not require the whole nation to be rabidly antisemitic: while many Germans were aware that Jews were being persecuted, and many knew about the systematic killings, many were unaware. Among those who were aware, there were many who were more concerned about day-to-day worries, including the fate of family and friends in the ongoing war. Fourth, many of the front-line perpetrators of mass killings found their own involvement highly disturbing: heavy drinking among the perpetrators was a common occurrence. Most recently, Norman Ohler's book *Blitzed: Drugs in the Third Reich* has conclusively demonstrated not only that Hitler was highly dependent on drugs, but that these were also widely distributed to his armies to help immunize them against the dehumanizing effects of taking part in mass murder, and to keep them awake through long hours of marching and manning the camps. Katz shows how individuals can live with radically different ethical codes or 'moral universes', which makes it only too possible for people to be loving parents, dedicated scientists, and mass murderers at the same time.

After World War II, in which Germany suffered a devastating defeat, the 'scientific racism' which had underpinned Nazi ideology came under sustained criticism, which is explored in the next chapter.

Chapter 3
The demise of scientific racism

In the aftermath of the Holocaust and the ending of the World War II in 1945, the role of eugenics and scientific racism in underpinning the ideology of Nazism was impossible to ignore. Antisemitism was only one among several forces that eventually led to the murderous project to annihilate the Jews. But it was clear that the question of racism and its scientific basis had to be confronted at an international level as part of the attempt to build a successful post-fascist world order.

In July 1950, the newly established United Nations Scientific and Cultural Organization (UNESCO) published a statement that challenged the credibility of scientific racism. The effect of this statement has to be understood in the context of the times. This was a period when, whatever the misgivings about Nazism as a political project, there was widespread popular and academic acceptance of a scientific foundation for the division of humankind into separate races with different, stable, biologically inherited characteristics.

While the UNESCO announcement may have come as a bolt from the blue for large numbers of people, the scientific grounding for this challenge had in fact been in preparation for some time *before* the Holocaust. The interwar period had been characterized by a growing scepticism towards scientific racism. In the USA it came primarily from the newly expanding field of cultural anthropology. In the UK the critique emerged largely from biology and other natural sciences.

Studies by the American anthropologist Franz Boas and his students reanalysed IQ tests conducted by the American army and showed that in fact northern blacks had outperformed southern whites. They also undermined the belief in the existence and significance of 'pure' races. Anthropomorphic measurements and detailed genealogies were conducted, which showed that hybrid populations resulting from 'mixture' between blacks and whites displayed a homogeneity which was even greater than that found among those of 'pure' European descent.

However, despite the revulsion against Nazi versions of scientific racism, and the new critical voices of the 1930s, it is worth remembering that during the war African American troops had been segregated from white soldiers, their blood supplies were kept separately, and *The Races of Mankind*, a pamphlet in which the anthropologist Ruth Benedict had challenged the idea of white superiority, was banned in the armed forces. Segregation was widely practised in the southern states in schooling and jobs, and diminished the electoral registration of black Americans. In Europe, many Italians were in the grip of ideas about the superiority of the Roman race that had supposedly produced the Roman Empire—and there were plenty of Nazi supporters in Germany. The Japanese, moreover, had made claims to be the master race of Asia.

But throughout the post-1950 period the work of biologists and social scientists continued to undermine the scientific claims of the category of race.

One key difficulty that exposed the lack of scientificity of the concept was that practically each racial scientist came up with a bewildering classification of human races. For instance, in 1933 von Eickstedt had come up with a scheme which included three main races, eighteen sub-races, three 'collateral' races, and three 'intermediate' types.

As the early opponents of the concept in the 1930s had pointed out, and as indeed Darwin had done much earlier, whatever the criteria used, the concept of race simply refused to provide unambiguously different types. To put it differently, no 'pure' races could be identified.

The fall of scientific racism

By the 1970s and 1980s, the concept of 'phenotype'—which refers to surface features of humans such as skin colour, shape of nose, texture of hair, shape and size of skull, and so forth—on which those attempting to develop a tenable concept of race and a hierarchy of races had relied, had been compellingly refuted as a guide to genuine human variation. Genetic research into underlying 'genotypes', based on genetic analysis, had demonstrated that there was negligible variation between humans. Moreover, the research conclusively showed that for any given population that had previously been differentiated from another group as a different 'race', there was more genetic variety *within* these groups than *between* them.

In 1972, a widely influential and compelling study by Richard Lewontin had concluded that there was only a 15 per cent genetic variation across 'racially' and geographically classified populations. Lewontin was able to conclude, emphatically, that 'the largest part of human variation . . . [is] accounted for by differences between individuals. Hence racial classification is of no social value and is positively destructive of social and human relations.'

The rapid development of research into human DNA and the decoding of the whole human genome, which was completed in 2000, confirmed the earlier genetic research. 'Genetics' has been replaced by 'genomics', a much more precise and scientifically revealing study of variation in human populations, although the earlier term is also commonly used for the same type of research. In June 2000 the first results of the human genome research project were announced at a White House ceremony led by President Clinton. A pioneer of DNA sequencing research, Craig Venter, was able to confirm then what earlier genetic research had shown: 'The concept of race has no genetic or scientific basis.'

Genomics has advanced rapidly. Among many other things, we now know that every human individual has the same collection of genes and, with the exception of identical twins, each individual has a *slightly* different version of *some* of these genes. We also now know that *all* humans are descended from an original population in Africa.

Anatomically, human beings originated in Africa, and there may have been several northward migrations from southern and central Africa from as long as 270,000 years ago, possibly driven by severe droughts. More modern Africans, from whom we are all descended, migrated out of Africa some 60,000 years ago, carrying with them only a small fraction of the genetic diversity of the original African population. Not surprisingly, the greatest genetic variation is to be found in Africa, whose populations have more genetic variation than those of all the other continents combined.

Moreover, contrary to common-sense assumptions about African phenotypical similarities—Africans are often all regarded as being 'black' and having flat noses and thick lips—in fact this is far from being the case. Anthropologists have demonstrated that even in a single region of Africa, for example what is now called the Ivory Coast, there are differences that are easily visible—in skin colour, from light brown to very much darker shades; in nose form, from flat to aquiline; and in hair colour as well—and these differences are even more striking when the whole of sub-Saharan Africa is systematically examined.

Africa contains the most variation in the world in physical type due to the vast variety of genetic heritage. It has the shortest and tallest people, populations with the thickest and thinnest lips, and very wide differences in the widths of noses and skull dimensions. Populations thought to consist of a single 'tribe' show a continuous grading of gene frequencies, while populations thought to be biologically separate have much greater genetic similarity than previously thought. The genetic diversity of Africa is often regarded as analogous to the fact that its population speaks 2,000 different languages.

Changes in genes are the result of random human mutations, and when these mutations enhance human survival in any given environment, they have a greater propensity to be transmitted to later generations, although there are still some phenotypical variations that cannot yet be explained in this manner. For example, if groups are separated for long periods, it is more likely that they will exhibit greater genetic variation between them, but within the strict limits that still define all the populations as belonging to a common human species.

The recent development of a method for extracting DNA from ancient bones reveals that the migrant populations out of Africa mixed with Neanderthals (no such mixing is evident among remaining, present-day Africans) and reached Australia between 42,000 and 65,000 years ago. However, the first major areas of settlement appear to have been in Arabia, Persia, and subsequently India. Settlement in Europe seems to have taken place around 50,000 years ago, later than in what is present-day China. South America was probably populated about 15,000 years ago.

'Cheddar Man' and variation in skin colour and other features among humans

In February 2018 scientists unveiled a sculpture of the first modern Britons. They had lived about 10,000 years ago and the DNA analysis of the skeleton, which had in fact been unearthed more than a hundred years ago in Gough's Cave, in the Cheddar Gorge area of Somerset, revealed that these Britons were far from the light-skinned, straight- and fair-haired humans that they had been supposed to be.

'Cheddar Man' had 'dark to black skin', curly dark hair, and blue eyes (see Figure 5). He was part of an original population that had been the first settlers who had crossed from continental Europe to Britain at the end of the last ice age, and 10 per cent of white British people alive today are descended from this group.

The DNA results suggested a Middle Eastern origin for Cheddar Man. Scientists believe that European populations became lighter skinned over time to enable them to produce enough vitamin D,

5. **Cheddar Man.**

although it should be noted that protection against skin cancer involves far more complex mechanisms than the darker pigmentation produced by melanin.

It is likely that the dark-skinned Cheddar Man was a hunter-gatherer and was able to make sharp flint blades, harpoons for fishing, and bows and arrows.

Light skin does not have its sole origins in Europe. DNA analysis suggests that it is more likely that it developed first in Asia and only then spread to Europe. Africa is also the source of other gene variants that contribute to lighter skin in human populations around the world.

It is hardly surprising that Tom Booth, an archaeologist at the Natural History Museum, argues that the racial categories so beloved of 'race' scientists of the 18th, 19th, and 20th centuries simply have not existed from time immemorial. The 'racial types' they posited are of relatively recent origin, having been replaced over and over by other types of populations in previous centuries.

Yoan Diekmann, a computational biologist from University College London, who worked on the project to sequence and decode the DNA of 'Cheddar Man', pointed out that their research project had demonstrated that there was no necessary connection between whiteness and Britishness (the same applies to Europeanness).

It may appear surprising that only 10 per cent of the current British population derives from the hunter-gatherer 'Cheddar Man'. However, as Reich, one of the pioneers of the science of extracting DNA from ancient bones, points out, 'we now know from ancient DNA, that people who live in a particular place today almost never exclusively descend from the people who lived in the same place in the past'. Although European hunter-gatherers had the dark skin and blue eyes of 'Cheddar Man', Reich points out that the first European farmers had light skin but dark hair and brown eyes, 'thus light skin in Europe largely owes its origins to migrating farmers', probably from eastern Siberia, although it is probable that Asia figures in the mix.

Reich's conclusion, relating to the idea of purity of 'race' (and by implication, 'nation', as we shall see), is worth citing in full:

> By demonstrating that the genetic fault lines in West Eurasia between ten and fifteen thousand and four thousand years ago were entirely different from today's, the ancient DNA revolution has shown that today's classifications do not reflect fundamental pure units of biology. Instead, today's divisions are recent phenomena, with their origin in repeating mixtures and migrations. The findings of the ancient DNA revolution suggest that the mixtures will continue. *Mixture is fundamental to who we are, and we need to embrace it, not deny that it occurred.* (Emphasis added)

For instance, Reich and his fellow researchers have discovered that the Han Chinese, the world's largest group with a size of 1.2 million, derived from a wide range of population groups. The Han unified China in 202 BCE, but share many genetic similarities with the population of Tibet. However, most crucially, both 'harboured large proportions of their ancestry from a population that no longer exists in unmixed form', and could be excluded from having contributed ancestry to many South-East Asian populations.

'Race', culture, and nation

With regard to the common-sense idea of nations having ancient roots, DNA research on India, for example, suggests that the Hindutva ideology espoused by various extremist Hindu organizations associated with the ruling Bharatiya Janata Party (in power at the time of writing), is, to put it bluntly, simply false. Hindutva ideologies are not monolithic: some are more cultural, others more racial. But common to them is the notion of a very ancient Hindu population that is thousands of years old, whose unity has only been disturbed by Muslim invasions and British Christian colonial rule.

The ancient DNA evidence reveals a different set of formations of the Indian population. One important argument of many who espouse the Hindutva ideology claims that the ancient civilizations based around the walled cities of Harappa and Mohenjo-daro, which existed from approximately 4,500 to 3,800 years ago, demonstrate the existence of an unbroken Hindu population. But their script, which has not yet been decoded, shows no resemblance to Sanskrit, the Indo-European language which forms the basis of Indian languages and those of Iran and Europe.

Another of the great mysteries that remains is why these Indus Valley civilizations declined. The Nazis deployed a common notion of an Indo-Aryan invasion from the north, which suited their view that the real origins of all European languages lay in the lands of north-eastern Europe, including Germany, and their ambition was to replicate what they regarded as militaristic expansion by the populations from these lands.

Hindutva ideologues have been particularly critical of any such notion, for it suggests that crucial elements of Indian culture have their origins outside South Asia. They have a point. There is little archaeological evidence of a mass migration during a relatively short period.

However, genetic evidence definitely suggests a more gradual mixture, dating from the decline and fall of Harappa. This is reinforced by the archaeological evidence that the Indus Valley civilizations did not use horses, although they were used by populations after the end of these cultures. The genetic mixture of

Indians consists of individuals and groups of West Eurasian and Near Eastern origin, and a quite different population, a finding reinforced by the fact that Indians in the south of the subcontinent speak Dravidian languages.

Reich and his Indian co-researchers have come to the conclusion that 'everyone in mainland India today is a mix, albeit in different proportions…No group in India can claim genetic purity.' The West Eurasian, Near Eastern, and Caucasian mixture of those who have more relation to 'Ancestral North India' demonstrates that the idea of a pure Hindu population or, for some, 'race', is completely untenable. And what goes for Indians goes for all groups that 'race' scientists have attempted to classify as 'pure' in racial terms.

'Black' and 'white' in America

Given the complexity of the formation of white and black Americans, it is not surprising that the 'African' in African American is seldom 'pure' African. The *National Geographic* magazine published a special 'Race' issue in April 2018. Using a specially designed kit, they tested six individuals who self-identified in a variety of ways, but always with the awareness that they had some African ancestry. The results showed that all the individuals, who look quite different, had the same ancestral mix: 32 per cent northern European, 28 per cent southern European, 21 per cent sub-Saharan African, and 14 per cent South-West Asian/North African. One, Brenda Yurkoski, now living in Virginia, knew before the test that her set of ancestors included President Thomas Jefferson and his black slave mistress Sally Hemings. The fact of this relationship has also been confirmed by DNA research. Note that Brenda Yurkoski self-identifies as African American, but the others often use 'mixed race'.

Race and health

Particular diseases have often been associated with distinct population groups. But none of the relevant research findings support the idea of separate *races*. Thalassemia, often regarded as being most common in those from the Indian subcontinent, is known to occur with great frequency in some Mediterranean regions and South-East Asia as well.

Sickle cell anaemia is often thought to be an 'African' or 'black' affliction. But research points to a correlation not with 'race', however defined, but with the presence of malaria in an environment. Populations with sickle cell disease appear to have been more likely to survive malaria epidemics, and the genetic predisposition to sickle cell disease was thus passed down the generations. There is little evidence to suggest that the disease originated in West Africa, and it is not solely confined to those who are phenotypically 'black'. Sickle cell disease also occurs among populations with Indian, Arabian, Greek, Turkish, and Italian ancestry.

Osteoporosis is one among a host of other significant examples that have been used to shore up the view that humans can be meaningfully divided into distinct races. In biomedical literature 'Caucasians' and 'Asians' are regarded as having greater propensity to the disease. But this is not a *racial* divide: 'Asian' is a geographical category, while the idea of 'Caucasian' as a distinct group, as we have seen earlier, has always mixed up biology, geography, and culture.

The confusion here is a product of lack of intellectual rigour, which results in an illegitimate conflation between *biological differentiation on some dimensions* with the vocabulary of *racial* genetics.

What research into diseases confirms is the view that humankind does indeed have populations with distinct commonalities of ancestral gene pools, resulting from interbreeding and particular migratory flows. But the pattern of distribution of pools and physiological features simply does not support the idea of separate races.

'Ancestry is not a euphemism, nor is it synonymous with "race"', as Reich points out. Although the genomics revolution so far has revealed that there are 'nontrivial' average genetic differences between populations, across a whole range of traits, 'the race vocabulary is too ill-defined and too loaded with historical baggage to be helpful'. Thus, although there are well-established average differences between populations—in terms of skin colour, the ability to effectively digest starch or lactose, the ability to thrive more easily at high altitudes, and susceptibility to some diseases—Lewontin's earlier conclusion still stands: *variation for the majority of traits is much greater within than between populations.*

Let us take just one example which is symptomatic of the complexities involved when claims are made about genetic differences that help some groups to excel at particular sports or athletic activities. It is often asserted that living in the Kenyan Highlands has given athletes from this region a genetic advantage in long-distance running. But Tibetans also walk and run at high altitudes without developing the same abilities as Kenyan runners. Examples of this type can be multiplied many times over, demonstrating that the relation between genes, environment, and behavioural traits simply does not support the idea of separate races.

And it bears repeating that DNA evidence of constant migratory flows and turnovers of populations leads to the indubitable conclusion that most of today's population groups are not exclusively the descendants of people who lived in the same regions as little as 10,000 years ago.

A more recent development in the biological sciences is *epigenetics*, and many commentators, such as Maurizio Meloni, are concerned that attempts are already being made to smuggle in the concept of 'race' via this new form of research and theorization. Epigenetics is usually defined as the study of changes in gene function that do not entail a change in the sequence of DNA. The danger that lurks in this seemingly harmless form of DNA analysis lies in its claim that the environment of humans can affect the *expression* of genes, such that the foetus in the womb may be affected by trauma experienced by the mother. Moreover, the effect is allegedly one that might last generations.

One of the best-known hypotheses in epigenetics with regard to 'race' is the so-called 'slavery hypothesis', which suggests that the phenomenon of a greater likelihood of low birth weight of African American babies compared to white American babies over several generations is the result of poor nutrition and oppressive working conditions experienced by the previous generation of mothers under slavery, which has genetic effects that are passed on. This view is buttressed by the finding that present-day women of African origin living in the USA, from what were previously regions where slaves were recruited, give birth to babies with significantly higher weight than African American mothers whose ancestral mothers had experienced slavery. A further argument has also been made that the children of mothers whose ancestors experienced the trauma of the Holocaust show the epigenetic effects of the trauma.

Of course, were this form of genetic explanation to be true, it would also support the argument that improving resources for African American women could trigger epigenetic changes that would be beneficial, and in principle this could apply not just to health but to other performance indicators.

However, at present there are three serious problems for a reinvigoration of the concept of race via epigenetics. One is that there is little understanding of the mechanisms, even if they exist, of how environmental factors interact with gene expression; furthermore, the mechanisms of intergenerational transmission of these genetic changes are even less well understood. Third, there is scant evidence that epigenetic differences mirror any systematic *racial* classification of groups. Epigenetics is a discipline that relies more on speculation than genuine scientific understanding. Nevertheless, scholars of race and racism would do well to keep a wary eye on epigenetic research, as this is an avenue whereby many researchers will attempt to resurrect the biological concept of race.

Defining 'race': is there a consensus that race is a social construct?

Most sociologists in the UK and many in the USA are now convinced by scientific research that 'race' is a social construct rather than a biological fact. This is often reflected in the use of quotation marks around race by sociologists, and indeed I often follow this practice here and in other writings (although my usage in this book varies). In addition, they are likely to emphasize that the concept of race has been deployed, more often than not—as confirmed by the historical survey presented earlier in this book— as an ideology in projects of group or, more appropriately, 'racial' dominance. Thus sociologists tend to argue that in most forms of classification 'races' are hierarchically ordered, placing whites at the top and the darkest skinned peoples with other non-European features at the bottom. These hierarchies, it is argued, are used to justify racialized inequalities and to discriminate against these groups, say African Americans or Asians, in the provision of educational resources, the allocation of housing, the admission to institutions of higher education, the provision of employment opportunities, hiring practices, and so forth.

But how widespread is this view of 'race' as a social construct outside the academic cultures of sociology and biology? Any cosy complacency about the widespread discrediting of the concept of race is easily punctured. For the USA, significant interview and textual research conducted by the anthropologist Ann Morning suggests that not only are a great many academic anthropologists and even biologists still adhering to a biologically 'essentialist' concept of race, but this is also common among her sample of American undergraduates taking anthropology and biology courses. 'Essentialism' denotes the view that members of a group share one or more defining characteristics which are innate and unalterable. Her survey of popularly used biology and anthropology textbooks in US schools also demonstrates that there is a widespread tendency to use a biological concept of race rather than presenting students with the idea of race as a social construct.

Undoubtedly this is one important reason why the belief in biologically discrete 'races' has such a hold in popular culture, as reflected in studies of common-sense beliefs in the USA (and in European societies), although evidence of views as to a systematic hierarchy of races is, at best, patchy. Most ordinary people in the USA and in European societies tend to hold a vague notion of race, which they would only think about if pointedly asked about it, say in sociological or anthropological research. There has, however, been little research into lay concepts of 'race' in European societies, including, at the time of writing, the UK.

Moreover, as Ann Morning argues, and in contrast to what might have been expected, the genomic revolution might have actually served to reinforce a popular view of differentiated races because a great many people, in an age of growing diversity in the USA and Europe, are aware that skin colour and other phenotypical features shade into each other or appear in an incongruous manner—for example, many Asians of Chinese origin have flat noses, associated with those of African heritage, but straight hair—but are able to hold the view that under the surface, genetic differences revealed by the biological sciences confirm the view that races definitely exist. Nicholas Wade's book *A Troublesome Inheritance*, which claims to find a classification of biologically based 'races' in the latest research in genetics, is no doubt only the first of many books that will attempt to derive a concept of race from developments in the biological sciences.

Other significant reasons for this belief are, first, the continuing view, held by many medical researchers, that some diseases are genetically more likely in certain groups, and second the targeting by pharmaceutical companies of drugs which they claim are more appropriate for certain genetically defined groups. Perhaps the most widely known example of such a drug is BiDil, which was endorsed in 2005 by the US Food and Drug Administration as being particularly effective in treating heart failure in black patients. However, the research supporting this recommendation was seriously flawed because the clinical study only focused on self-identified blacks, thus failing to provide any means for a direct comparison with its efficacy in groups identifying racially in a different manner. As Morning points out, 'race'-specific drugs are constantly being promoted and thus will have a continuing influence in reinforcing the view that discrete races are identifiable under the skin, so to speak. Subsequent research by Morning, and Angela Saini, has confirmed that attempts are being made, albeit with dubious reasoning, to reintroduce the concept of race into science. Saini's book *Superior: The Return of Racial Science* is an excellent guide to the survival and contemporary revival of racial science.

Chapter 4
Racialization, cultural racism, and religion

Few people today, outside the ranks of hardcore members of neo-Nazi and other ultra-right-wing groups, admit to being *racist*. However, even self-confessed racists appear to have little agreement about how many races exist and how exactly they are to be differentiated from each other. The supporters of the concept of race in the past had exactly the same difficulty and, as we have seen, the proliferation of schemas of racial classification was one reason for the demise of 'scientific racism'.

The afterlife of 'race'

However, as I argued at the end of Chapter 3, the idea of 'race' has a strong afterlife, especially in white-dominated societies.

Popular culture in the USA is suffused with 'race' and racial thinking. The republic was founded on the racial assumption that blacks were not to be regarded as citizens. The original document of the American Constitution states that for purposes of representation in Congress, a slave was to be counted as 'three-fifths' of a white inhabitant of the state. This was arrived at as a compromise solution to the problem that if slaves were regarded as full persons, the southern states would have had a disproportionate representation in Congress. Discussions of the 'Negro' question—as it used to be called even by African

Americans until the slide from 'Negro' to 'nigger' was halted by the civil rights movements of the 1960s—has thus been part and parcel of official and everyday discussion, and the US census explicitly uses a racial classification, as do schools, hospitals, and other national and state-level institutions. Morning describes the relief with which she realized, when about to give birth to her second child in Italy, having had her first in the USA, that the ubiquitous question of her 'race' was simply never asked.

In the UK, with its long imperial and colonial history, which included slavery, race thinking was embedded in notions of British imperialism as a 'civilizing' project and as the 'white man's burden'. This also, of course, served to mask the fact that imperialism and colonialism were essentially forms of exploitation from which Britain profited enormously. Popular representations of race, especially in the idea of blackness as a form of dirt, were long perpetuated in advertisements for soap as being so effective that it could even clean and 'whiten' dirty black skins (Figure 3). School textbooks and popular children's and adult fiction from the last quarter of the 19th century and into the 20th century presented white heroes 'discovering' new lands in Africa and Asia, subduing 'savages' and 'primitive' populations, and bringing to them superior white British and European civilization. The idea that colonization was basically a good thing, bringing modern technology and better forms of government, is still widespread, although this is truer of older people. The idea that India was 'given' railways, for example, is one often encountered by this author, and by many others, and the riposte that railways were primarily built to better aid the importation and diffusion of British goods at the expense of Indian industry (most recently exposed in Shashi Tharoor's book *Inglorious Empire*) is met with considerable resistance and even disbelief, even by white British university students taught by the author.

The arrival of black and Asian immigrants in the period after World War II (beginning with the steamship the SS *Windrush* in

1948 carrying some 800 West Indians), which brought much needed labour to rebuild the British economy, caused a variety of social panics, including within governments that nevertheless were forced to actively recruit in the colonies after labour supplied by Poles and other Europeans who had settled here during the war dried up. Enoch Powell, who was later notorious for wanting to expel 'coloured' immigrants, had in fact actively recruited West Indian nurses while minister of health in the 1960s, while the British Ministry of Transport also eagerly promoted the recruitment of West Indians, Indians, and Pakistanis to man the buses. Others were encouraged to come to fill low-skilled manufacturing jobs, especially in motor car and textile factories.

However, the arrival of 'coloureds' unleashed the powerful currents of overt racism in Britain that had been long in the making. The new arrivals faced appalling racism, especially in their attempts to find housing. The 'no dogs, no Irish, no coloureds' signs that festooned potential lodgings soon became infamous manifestations of this racism. The language of 'race' was a potent force in British politics, inscribed in a by-election slogan in the winning candidate's campaign in Smethwick in the West Midlands in 1964, which famously read, 'If you want a nigger for a neighbour, vote Labour'.

The racialization of language in the UK was perpetuated by the British habit of referring to relations between growing ethnic minority populations and the white British as an issue of 'race relations'. This discourse was codified in a series of Race Relations Acts in 1965, 1968, and 1976, which finally attempted to thwart overt and then covert discrimination on the grounds of 'race'.

Note, too, the phenomenon of 'banal nationalism', as signalled by Mick Billig in the title of his book. Billig highlights the manner in which symbols of nationalism are part of the fabric of everyday life. The flying of the national flag, the Union Jack, as a routine matter of course; celebrations of royal weddings and milestones in the monarch's reign as *national* 'jubilees'; memorial ceremonies for those killed in wars defending the nation; the retelling of national victories in epic historical battles, especially in films about the defeat of Nazi Germany in 1945; and supporting the national team and individuals in matches and tournaments. All inculcate a habitual form of nationalism and also a notion of the world as 'naturally' divided into nations, each with a distinct homeland and language, and a variety of long-established cultural characteristics embedded in national stereotypes.

However, given the close affinity between notions of 'nation' and 'race', it is hardly surprising that it becomes possible to label immigrants and foreigners not just as national others, but as *racial* others. Debates about immigration, as for example in the 2016 events leading up to the 'Brexit' referendum (Britain voting on whether to leave the European Union), were suffused with messages about race and belonging, most famously in a picture of Nigel Farage, a prominent 'Leave' supporter, in which his image is shown on a billboard with a long line of brown figures in the background wanting to enter Europe. The impression of brown hordes just waiting to invade 'white' Europe illegally was definitely conveyed. This chimed well with the racialized alarms set off by the Leave campaign's claim that Turkey was imminently going to join the European Union and Turks would be free to enter Europe, including the UK. Of course, the message was mixed up with what has come to be called 'Islamophobia', which is discussed later in this chapter, but the point here is that the notion of a world 'naturally' divided into nations makes it that much easier to elide 'nation' into 'race', especially if the cultures and 'values' of other nations, especially 'non-white nations' or Muslim nations, are represented as being intrinsically incommensurable with 'our' values and 'way of life'.

A tragic consequence of a panic around immigration during the Brexit campaigns—it is difficult to establish a watertight causal link, of course, although there was a febrile anti-immigration national atmosphere at the time—was the murder of British MP Jo Cox (a prominent campaigner for Syrian and other refugees) by Thomas Mair, a white man with connections to extreme right-wing groups such as the National Front and the English Defence League. Mair shouted 'Britain first' during the murder, and believed that Jo Cox was a 'traitor to the white race'. In court, the judge described the convicted killer as a 'white supremacist'. Note, especially, the elision between 'National', 'Britain', 'English', and 'white' that is represented by the groups to which he was linked and that he expressed in his outbursts. Here we see a tragic equivalence being made between 'the British or English nation' and the white 'race'.

Defining 'race' and 'ethnicity' in official discourses

A clear definition of race would seem to be crucial if claims that a racist act has occurred are to be rigorously substantiated. Nowhere is this more vital than in anti-racist legislation, including in the UK, where such anti-discriminatory laws have been defined as Race Relations Acts, as we have seen.

How can race be defined in a context where *racial* discrimination is the target, but where it is also accepted that 'race' has no scientific foundation?

Let us begin with a defining case. In 1978, in Britain, under the 1976 Race Relations Act, the parents of a Sikh boy, Gurinder Singh Mandla, sued Park Grove, a private school in Birmingham. The school had refused entry to the boy on the grounds that his turban contravened school uniform rules. In 1983 the House of Lords ruled in favour of the Mandlas.

In particular, in this landmark ruling, it was deemed that Sikhs were a *racial* group because they had a long, shared history; cultural traditions of their own; a common geographical origin (or descent from a small number of common ancestors); a common language; a common literature; a common religion; and they were a minority or a majority within a larger community. The House of Lords also argued that a person was a member of a racial group if he or she regarded himself or herself as a member and was accepted as such.

The House of Lords judgment raises a number of difficult issues that are endemic in attempts to provide credible modern definitions of racism, both in legal and other contexts.

Most crucially, the judgment used primarily *cultural* criteria to define a *racial* group, rather than features such as skin colour. It also included the idea of voluntary self-definition, which introduces an extraordinary arbitrariness.

One key difficulty with an exclusively *cultural* definition of a *racial* group is that it makes it impossible to differentiate from the modern idea of *ethnicity*. But ethnicity, too, is a problematic concept. *Ethnic* and *ethnicity* derive from the Greek *ethnos*, which refers to a people, a group sharing certain common cultural attributes. In its modern usage ethnicity assumes the possession of a relatively high degree of coherence and solidarity among a group of people who have a conception of common origins, shared culture and experiences, and common interests, and who participate in some shared activities in which common origin and culture are regarded as significant.

However, as anthropologists, sociologists, and historians have discovered, it is difficult to identify which cultural attributes and shared activities can be taken to define common ethnicity. For example, how important is a common language, and how is this to be weighed against the possession of a common religion?

And what is to count as a common religion? On some criteria common adherence to Christianity or Islam may be enough. However, in Iraq, Pakistan, and other Muslim countries there is a significant division between Sunni and Shi'a Muslims. In Northern Ireland, despite the commonality of Christianity and the English language, divisions between Protestant and Catholic versions of Christianity, overlain with significant political divisions partly stemming from Cromwell's annexation of Ireland in the 17th century and his policy of settling Protestants there, have fuelled political and armed conflicts between the two white populations.

Ethnicity, like race, is above all a matter of drawing boundaries around zones of *belonging* and *non-belonging*. These include, therefore, *subjective* elements of identity construction, processes of *identification* with particular groups, as well as responses to labels of identity and difference imposed from outside, as in the way Turkey's Muslim identity is emphasized by many in Europe and was used in the 2016 referendum on what has now come to be called Brexit.

Another major problem, however, is encountered by what social scientists call the *situational* and *contextual* nature of ethnic identity construction.

A female journalist from Wales reporting from India or the USA for a British newspaper may accept an Indian's or American's identification of her as 'English', but in Britain may want to emphasize the distinctness of her Welshness. In India, Africa, or the Middle East she may be willing to accept the label 'European', but she may be opposed to membership of the European Union on account of a strong belief in a distinctive British identity and national interests. In other contexts she may be willing to go along with external labels of her as a 'Westerner', although she may have weak subjective feelings of identification with this broad category.

In Britain today, many people of Pakistani, Muslim origin living in Glasgow identify themselves as 'Scottish Muslims', having absorbed Scottish feelings of animosity towards the English.

Others just call themselves Muslims, and have a strong sense of belonging to a global Muslim community or *umma* as their primary point of identification. Some Muslims, though, feel that they are British Muslims, or just British.

Social scientists now regard the stabilization of ethnic categories as a political process in the broadest sense: ethnic identities are constantly subject to formation and reformation and to contextual negotiation, and often involve mobilization in attempts to create political divisions.

Note too that in the examples I have cited there is no clear distinction made between ethnicity and nationality or sense of national belonging. 'Territoriality' or geographical boundaries are further sources of indeterminacy and negotiation in the formation of ethnicities.

Race, ethnicity, and national statistics classifications in the UK

And when 'race' enters the equation the result is a confusing melange of categories, as exhibited for example in the latest (2019) guidelines published by the UK Office for National Statistics, based on an elaboration of the 2011 Census; these categories, then, are not identical to but not dissimilar to the 2011 Census:

White
  White Irish
  White Gipsy/Traveller
  White other
Mixed
  Mixed White/Asian
  Mixed White/Black African
  Mixed White/Black Caribbean
  Mixed other

Asian
Bangladeshi
Chinese
Indian
Pakistani
Asian other
Black
Black African
Black Caribbean
Black other
Other
Arab
Any other

It is not difficult to identify here what is nowadays a chronic confusion in official public discourses and governmental monitoring schemes between *racial* categories such as black and white with *national* identities such as Indian and Pakistani, and the further problems created by the 'mixed' classifications that conflate racial (black and white) with geographical classifications such as Asian, Caribbean, and African. The Asian category also reveals the ambiguities involved in classifying the Chinese, who are allowed a place of their own. The British NHS had previously used the racial category 'Caucasian', but this has now been omitted.

And at least half a century's political struggles by subordinate groups have also left a significant imprint. 'Black', which up to the 1960s was a derogatory label, has been reappropriated and revalorized by the civil rights and Black Power movements in the USA. The slogan 'Black is Beautiful' empowered populations otherwise also reviled as 'niggers' and 'coloureds' in their struggle for civil rights.

In the UK in the 1970s and 1980s 'black' was adopted by anti-racist movements as part of a relatively successful political strategy to mobilize and unite diverse populations whose origins lay mainly in the Caribbean and South Asia. Among other things it showed up the racial assumptions of the term 'coloured', in common use even in the 1960s, which took *white*ness as a supposedly *colourless* and invisible norm with which to classify and discriminate against people from the Indian subcontinent and the West Indies.

On the other hand, the increasing educational, economic, political, and cultural fragmentation of the British minority populations in the last part of the 20th century is now also reflected in the need to include separate categories for populations of Indian, Pakistani, Bangladeshi, African, Caribbean, and Chinese origin.

Racism without 'race': initial explorations of 'hard', 'deracialized', and 'new' racism

By now the success of anti-racist campaigns in the USA and the whole of western Europe is also reflected in the moral opprobrium attached to the label 'racist'. Hence, in part, the reluctance of citizens and politicians to identify themselves openly as racist.

On the basis of the historical survey of the development of doctrines of 'race' presented in previous chapters, a widely accepted version of 'hard', 'strong', or 'classical' racism can be presented as follows, borrowed from a formulation by the noted anti-racist British biologist Steven Rose:

> By racism is meant any claim of the natural superiority of one identifiable human population, group, or race over another. By 'scientific racism' is meant the attempt to use the language and some of the techniques of science in support of theories or contentions that particular groups or populations are innately superior to others in terms of intelligence, 'civilisation' or other socially defined attitudes.

How easily such a broadly accepted definition can be sidestepped, and the accusation of racism avoided, can be seen in the following case study of Enoch Powell, a British politician who was widely accused of racism, especially after speaking in Parliament against the passing of the Race Relations Act of 1968 which attempted to legislate against racial discrimination, which he followed up with the now notorious 'rivers of blood' speech to his local Conservative group in Birmingham. The speech was so-called because Powell, using his knowledge of the classics (he had been a classics scholar), quoted, or, some claim, misquoted, from the *Aeneid* in describing the long-term effects of 'coloured immigration': 'like the Roman, I seem to see "the River Tiber foaming with much blood"'.

The rhetoric of racism and disavowal: the case of Enoch Powell

Asked in 1969 whether he was a racist, Powell replied: 'if by racialist you mean a man who despises a human being because he belongs to another race, or a man who believes that one race is inherently superior to another in civilisation or capability for civilisation, then the answer is emphatically no'.

Powell's denial that he was *racist*, though somewhat disingenuous in ways we shall explore, nevertheless also has a sound and credible basis, if we accept Rose's widely accepted definition of racism cited earlier.

Powell, by jettisoning any claims to *natural* and *innate* superiority and inferiority between human groups, immediately distanced himself from forms of thinking that have been taken to be central to racism.

Interestingly, Powell refered not to *racism* but to *'racialism'*, and appeared to endorse the existence of 'races' as naturally bounded populations. Many scientists and social scientists have argued that any doctrine which accepts that races really exist as naturally bounded populations is thereby racist. On this criterion, Powell would appear to be endorsing at least part of what many commentators would include in a definition of racism.

But it is also the case that by denying any belief in innate superiority and inferiority between races, and also by claiming that there is no warrant for any race despising another, Powell is able to rebut the accusation of racism, or so it seems.

But this is only on the basis of one quotation. It therefore becomes necessary to see Powell's disavowal of racism in the context of the whole speech, an examination of his other statements of belief, and his practices such as vocal interventions in parliamentary debates.

In the speech, Powell presents himself as a defender of the English nation, and as one who spoke a truth that had been articulated by ordinary people in his constituency, but which was being ignored by liberal politicians. The speech constructs a framework for his listeners and readers in which the victim is not the immigrant who is discriminated against and who might be protected from this by the Race Relations Act. The real victims of allowing an invasion of 'coloured' people were ordinary, decent, hard-working English people who now found it difficult to find beds in hospitals and places for their children in schools, people who indeed now found a form of constructing victimhood that was also very apparent during the Brexit campaign. White British, he claimed, were now becoming *strangers in their own land*, a portentous phrase much used subsequently by those wanting to advocate some or other sort of exclusionary policy towards immigrants and other 'others'.

In his speech Powell uses an anecdote from an anonymous constituent, a war widow whose sons had also died during World War II, who was facing destitution. Powell's rhetorical strategy is worth noting: he avoids any mention of the West Indians and Indians who had fought alongside British forces against the Nazis, but does mention that the reason why she was facing destitution was that she refused to rent rooms to immigrant families. He regarded this as a perfectly legitimate form of discrimination that the forthcoming Race Relations Act would make a punishable act. *In other words, Powell was defending blatant racial discrimination against 'coloured' British people*, and this is in keeping with his general view, that people of different races should not be allowed to mix, indeed, that they could not mix. Elsewhere, Powell stated that 'racial' integration would be well-nigh impossible, because 'the West Indian does not by being born in England, become an Englishman. In law, he becomes a United Kingdom citizen by birth; *in fact he is a West Indian or an Asian still*' (emphasis added). In other words, Asians and West Indians have a (biological?) 'essence' that should keep them permanently apart from white British populations.

Thus, it is only by examining a whole host of contextual elements that the strength of Powell's racism becomes evident. And this is also why I have taken the view in this book that attempting to provide short, supposedly watertight and easily applied definitions of racism are misleading and fail to capture the full rhetorical features of racist statements and beliefs. Moreover, they would have to include definitions of racist actions by individuals or groups, which in turn raise complex questions of intention and motive, which a subsequent Race Relations Act passed in 1976 attempted to confront by introducing the notion of 'indirect racism'.

The case of Powell also supports my view that examining a single racist utterance does not allow us to conclude that the person is or is not racist. One has to look at further statements, as well as to actions, to establish whether a person has a strongly formed racist identity or whether racism is an occasional and contextual expression. In the case of Powell, his various statements, his opposition to a piece of legislation that would make overt racial discrimination illegal, his opposition to 'race mixing', and his description of black youth, in his 'rivers of blood' speech, as 'piccaninnies' is evidence of a strong and inflexible racist identity.

However, it is also worth adding how the notion that Asians and West Indians have a racial 'essence' that will never be diluted can slip over into a form of racial *dehumanization*: the British comedian Bernard Manning often joked that just as a dog does not become a horse by being born in a stable, so Asians and blacks do not become English by being born in England. That dogs and horses are different *species* means that Manning's joke slides implicitly into a strong form of biological racism, implying that Asians and blacks are different species from whites. Manning's utterances chillingly recall the claim by Goebbels, one of Hitler's henchmen, that the 'fact that the Jew lives among us is no proof that he belongs with us, just as a flea does not become a domestic animal because it lives in the house'.

The close affinity between 'race' and 'nation' is demonstrated particularly strongly in the way that nationalist statements like Trump's 'make America great again' (which many have argued is a dog-whistle form of racism) also allude to a nostalgic 'make America *white* again', without actually spelling that out. The phrase 'America first' was adopted by the white supremacist Ku Klux Klan from an earlier isolationist slogan, and demonstrates how 'nation' can slide into racial discourse about 'whiteness' and the difficulty in simply labelling utterances as racist without an overall contextualization. The case of Thomas Mair, who murdered British MP Jo Cox in 2016 during the national campaigns to decide whether Britain should leave the European Union, discussed earlier, showed how his strong racism only becomes apparent when examined in relation to his other statements apart from 'Britain first' (which he shouted during the incident) and his active interest in white supremacist groups.

There are myriad instances of individuals who behave in a racist manner to some non-white groups, British Pakistanis for example, but not others, such as British Chinese. Wilhelm Marr, discussed earlier as one of the first to articulate the modern, racist, antisemitic doctrine of Jews as an undesirable race, in fact married Jewish women and eventually begged forgiveness from the Jewish nation.

The uses of racialization

It is in the context of difficulties of this type that the concept of racialization becomes useful. There have been a number of slightly varying usages of this concept, so it is important to set out how the notion is being used here. Usually the concept has been used to note that a topic, for example, paedophilia, has been racialized by explicitly linking it to ethnic minorities that have also commonly been seen as 'races', for example communities of Pakistani heritage, with the implication that they are the main perpetrators. My usage includes this sense of the concept, but is much wider. Racialization as deployed here acknowledges that propositions, insults, and more elaborate doctrines are liable to vary in the degree to which they contain elements of what I have called 'strong' or 'hard' (biological) racism, as encapsulated in the quotation from Steven Rose cited earlier. Exploring the degree to which propositions or utterances rest on strong biological or physiological differentiations between populations, and the extent to which ideas of innate superiority are overtly or covertly included, for example, allow a judgement to be made about the degree of racialization and racism. In this sense the concept adds much needed complexity to the blunt concept of 'racism', allowing for its multidimensionality.

It bears resemblance to the concept of 'racial formation' as used by sociologists Michael Omi and Howard Winant in their influential book, *Racial Formation in the United States*, with the latest edition being published in 2014. For Omi and Winant, and my view is to a considerable extent the same, 'race is an unstable and "decentred" complex of social meanings constantly being transformed by political struggle'.

The concept of racialization as used in the manner I am advocating moves research and political argument away from unproductive debates about whether any particular individuals, institutions, propositions, claims, and doctrines are *simply* 'racist' or 'non-racist'. Instead the debate is opened up to more useful analyses of the different mixes of biological and cultural connotations of difference, superiority, and inferiority that emerge in public or private acts, utterances, conversations, and jokes, or in justifications for discriminatory behaviour, for example in immigration legislation or hiring practices in workplaces. We can thus understand how social relations and ideas are *racialized*, as part of a broader racial frame of reference and racialized structures and institutions. Racism and racialization are *processes*, always 'works in progress', and liable to change and transformation from situation to situation, and during different historical periods. This usage of racialization becomes highly pertinent in my discussion of 'national populism' in the concluding section of the book.

It is my argument that in fact racialized utterances and the intentions underlying institutional practices usually contain a variable and complex mix of notions. Usually, biology and culture are variously combined within the 'race–nation–ethnicity complex'. This is a framework that is not necessarily well thought through by individuals having conversations or, say, hiring practices in institutions, and depending on the context can operate both explicitly and implicitly or in only one of these forms.

Racialization also does not imply that those who are subjected to it are necessarily regarded as inferior, although that is often the case. Thus, included are the not uncommon notions of cleverness that are often used with regard to Jews and the Japanese. And the application of covert quotas against Jews in the past with regard to admission into elite institutions of higher education, for example Harvard, for fear that they would gain a 'disproportionate' number of places, was no less racist for being based on the supposedly superior intelligence of these groups. Against Jews, Harvard has used non-academic criteria to limit their numbers, as documented in the sociologist Jerome Karabel's 2006 book *The Chosen: The Hidden History of Admission and Exclusion at Harvard, Yale and Princeton*.

What seem to be racist utterances or practices do not prove that the person or group making or involved in them intended them to be racist. Nor do they mean that the persons, groups, or institutions will always carry out such discriminatory actions or have done so in the past, nor that other groups that are racialized within the society will be treated in a similar manner. And the issue is made more complex by the recent deployment of the concept of *implicit bias*, which is considered later.

None of these issues is simply a matter of academic or research interest. It can become a vital issue in criminal trials. A remarkable incident that emerged in the trial of white youths accused of the racist murder of the black teenager Stephen Lawrence in 1993 in London aptly and tragically illustrates the importance and often intractability of this issue.

In order to gather evidence against the five white youths suspected of having committed the murder, police secretly filmed the suspects at home. The footage shows the young men shouting racist obscenities and play-acting with knives. But the film was not used as evidence. It would have been easy for the youths to argue in court, as they had done publicly, that they were only 'fooling around' or 'messing about', and that the incidents revealed nothing about their intentions or role in the murder of Stephen Lawrence.

The issue of the relationship between speech acts and other forms of discriminatory behaviour remains problematic, and inferences have to be made with close attention to context and other behavioural aspects or institutional practice. What might seem plausible at a common-sense level does not necessarily convince when judgments of proof beyond reasonable doubt have to be made.

Racialization, power, and prejudice

My discussion so far may have given the impression that racialization is a process that only operates at the level of culture and ideology. However, my view is very different. 'Race' has always been a component of power. And power is a social relation. Racialization is therefore intimately imbricated in institutions and structures and has a structural and institutional presence over long periods of time. Individual acts of discrimination, and in many cases simply inaction in dismantling racialized structures, often unconsciously, reproduce these structures of racialized social relations. This is the only way in which one can understand how structures of racialized inequality persist over very long periods of time, as we shall see in Chapter 5.

However, my view should not be understood as endorsing the formula common among many anti-racists that racism should be defined as 'power + prejudice'. There is an implication here that only those with 'power' may be regarded as racists. There are several problems with this thesis. With regard to power, who exactly may be said to possess power and how is power to be defined? One issue here is that the victim of power is *completely* powerless, but as many scholars have pointed out, even slaves exhibited various strategies of combating the power of their masters. If power is a social relation, the possession of it by one party to a relation does not necessarily deprive the other party of the power to resist. The difficulties that the 'prejudice + power' formula encounters are also apparent when the following question is asked: is it not possible for disadvantaged minorities in white societies to be 'racist'? In fact, there are many people of South Asian and Latino origin, occupying lowly positions in British and American society, who express virulently hostile attitudes towards people of African origin. A conception of racism that by its very definition rules out the notion that those with less power (the latter not being defined in the formula in any case) cannot be described as racists in white-dominated societies can be advanced, as we shall see, but requires careful argument. Moreover, how are poor whites to be characterized within this perspective? Whiteness does confer advantages, but again this requires careful, documented analysis. This issue is discussed in Chapter 5.

The concept of 'prejudice', as used in this formulaic manner of dealing with racism, is particularly problematic. Deriving from the academic disciplines of psychology and social psychology, the notion of prejudice carries strong connotations of ignorance and irrationality as properties of the 'prejudiced personality'. However, rectifying ignorance by factually undermining myths about blacks, other minorities, or indeed any human groups and individuals, can only work as an anti-racist strategy if the prejudiced person is open to rational argument, which by definition the irrational individual is not. More recently, there is considerable disquiet expressed about the concept of 'prejudice' in psychology and social psychology, as is evident in the contributions by social psychologists to the book *Beyond Prejudice*.

Cultural difference and the 'new racism'

The complex and multi-layered manner in which the category of 'race' now functions in the institutional and interpersonal relations within nation states and internationally has led many commentators to argue that it is necessary to speak not just of a single racism, but always to think of racisms in the plural, as mentioned earlier.

In this context, there has been considerable debate since the 1980s, especially in the UK, USA, and France, about a changing relationship between earlier, overt racism, and the emergence of a more covert racism that attempts to escape the opprobrium of open racism by omitting issues of *biology* altogether and focusing instead on questions of *culture* and ethnicity.

That is, there has been a growing belief that we have seen the development of a 'new racism'. This has been given a variety of labels: 'cultural racism', 'neo-racism', and 'the racism of cultural difference'.

There are good reasons for pursuing the 'new racism' debate, for it illuminates much about the way in which racialized discourses and practices have been evolving.

Race, cultural difference, and national identity: turning the tables on racism

> If we went on as we are, then by the end of the century there would be 4 million people of the New Commonwealth . . . here. Now that is an awful lot and I think it means that people are really rather afraid that this country might be swamped by people with a different culture. And, you know, the British character has done so much for democracy, for law, and done so much throughout the world, that if there is a fear that it might be swamped, people are going to react and be rather hostile to those coming in.
>
> Margaret Thatcher, leader of the Conservative Party, January 1978, interview given to Granada, *World in Action*

This is an interesting and important example of what has been called the *new racism*. But in what senses is it really racist? Or new?

In answering these questions we shall begin to unravel some of the complexities of changing discourses on race. And also, thereby, the difficulties of assigning clear-cut labels such as 'racist' and 'non-racist' to individuals or individual statements. *It is perhaps worth stating at the outset that what has been identified as the new racism places a greater emphasis on culture rather than biology* as a marker for racial difference.

Arguably, Thatcher's remarks are *not* racist in the following respects. They make no *direct* reference to 'race' nor to any 'racial' marker strongly associated with past racism, like skin colour, size of brain, or shape of nose. Indeed, the statements appear to be devoid of all biological referents and therefore seem very far from any form of what I have dubbed strong or classical (19th and first half of the 20th century) racism.

Nor is there an obvious reference to *superiority and inferiority* of peoples, especially with an underlying biological determinism—a staple of classical racism. Instead, and this in particular is what is supposedly new, the emphasis is on *cultural difference* and the genuine fears of ordinary citizens that their *national character* and, by implication, *way of life* may be in danger of being overwhelmed and marginalized.

However, note the strong contrast between *British national culture* and the character of outsiders from countries populated by *non-white* peoples. The 'New Commonwealth', in British political culture, has always functioned in a colour-coded manner by being contrasted with the predominantly white Old Commonwealth of Australia, New Zealand, and Canada.

Moreover, Thatcher singled out the British *nation* as a unique cultural formation. The *racial* significance of this reference is crucial. Historically, as we have seen, the concepts of nation and race have constantly been elided since the 18th century. Ideas of the 'nation' have consistently combined cultural, territorial, and biological proto-racial elements. Notions of distinct Anglo-Saxon, Germanic, Gallic, Slavic, and other racial cultures have strongly influenced ideas of unique British, German, French, and Russian national characteristics.

And *colour* and *culture* are strongly intertwined through chains of association in Thatcher's remarks. There is a strong implication that the brown and black New Commonwealth peoples lack commitment to democratic values and the rule of law. Moreover, they are portrayed as not having made a contribution to world history and global cultural achievements.

Thus connotations of biological, colour-based, nationally bounded cultural superiority and inferiority are strongly carried by the suggestion that democracy, the rule of law, and other contributions to global civilization have been made by British, and generally white—not New Commonwealth—peoples.

Of course, the white/non-white division and its association with democracy and other features is achieved by presenting a highly compressed and selective history of British imperialism in which brutal dispossession of land and resources, slavery, exploitation, and myriad massacres of non-white 'natives' in the Caribbean, Africa, and the Indian subcontinent are whitewashed out of the picture. Moreover, the fact that independent status was granted to the non-white colonies (and the USA) only after violent struggle, and democracy hastily and ineffectually installed prior to a swift exit, is also ignored. As is the suppression of democracy by white minority regimes of the time, such as Southern Rhodesia (Zimbabwe) and apartheid South Africa. It is well known that Thatcher was opposed to the imposition of sanctions against apartheid-era South Africa.

The extent to which Thatcher's claims are part of a deliberate, *intentional* obfuscation to hide possible racism is not easy to decipher, and this sort of question bedevils discussions of racism.

While the passage reproduced above manages to avoid explicit reference to 'race', Thatcher's attachment to the idea of race is openly exhibited in her rallying cry in 1982 in support of war with Argentina over the Falkland Islands, a sentiment immediately echoed in the *Times* newspaper:

> The people of the Falkland Islands, like the people of the United Kingdom, are an island race. Their way of life is British; their allegiance is to the Crown. (Margaret Thatcher, House of Commons, 3 April 1982)

> We are an island race, and the focus of attack is one of our islands, inhabited by islanders. (*The Times*, editorial, 5 April 1982)

These remarks are typical examples of the way in which, in more recent periods, race, nation, and culture ('way of life') can create effective chains of association.

Seen in this context, it is not possible to understand the way in which race now operates by only looking at single statements in isolation and deciding whether they are racist or not. Race operates in a whole variety of guises and with myriad taken-for-granted assumptions that have become embedded in public and private cultures in which ideas of nation, ethnicity, 'way of life', and other concepts have sometimes strong, sometimes less intense, racial connotations. The actual racism of statements such as those by Thatcher is a matter of complex and always debatable judgement.

Thatcher's remarks, arguably, can be regarded as a form of 'dog-whistle' appeals to racism, which Haney López, in his book *Dog Whistle Politics*, defines as 'coded racial appeals that carefully manipulate hostility towards non-whites . . . Superficially, these provocations have nothing to do with race, yet they powerfully communicate messages about threatening non-whites.'

How 'race' can trump 'culture'

The convenient way in which emphases can shift between various aspects of biology (or race) and nation or (culture) was evident at the time of these 1980s British debates over immigration by use of the notion of 'stock', suggesting that people of Asian and African Caribbean origin were not only culturally different but different from genuine British people who were regarded as being of Anglo-Saxon stock. Apart from excluding people of Jewish and Irish origin, this also had the unintended consequence of ignoring the huge impact of the 1066 Norman Conquest and settling of Britain, to mention just one of many movements of people into the British Isles.

'Anglo-Saxon' still functions as a shorthand descriptor for British peoples and institutions, creating a strong biological undercurrent for narratives of who does and does not legitimately belong to the nation.

Recent cases abound, of which I will mention only a few. When the 2017 engagement of Britain's Prince Harry to Meghan Markle, the 'mixed-race' American (her mother is African American), was announced, the partner of the then leader of the UK Independence Party was reported as stating that black people were ugly, that Prince Harry's fiancée would 'taint' the royal family, and that she probably had a 'tiny brain'. Leading newspapers, more circumspect about this sort of hard racism, confined themselves to coy references to Meghan Markle as not being the 'usual society blonde' that Prince Harry tended to date. After their baby was born on 6 May 2019, Danny Baker, a BBC radio presenter, was sacked for tweeting a photograph of a couple with a baby chimpanzee, titled 'Royal baby leaves hospital', although Baker claimed the photograph in the tweet, although 'a serious error of judgement', was a protest against privilege and not intended to be racist; the London Metropolitan Police declined to prosecute Baker on the grounds that Baker's tweet did not meet a 'criminal threshold'. In the USA, President Barack Obama and First Lady Michelle Obama were regularly compared to apes, again reviving a very old trope around biological dehumanization on which I remarked earlier. After they had left the White House, racist taunts continued, the best known so far being the tweet by the sitcom star Roseanne Barr in which she commented on former President Obama's senior adviser Valerie Jarret becoming a mother. Barr, using the abbreviation 'vj', tweeted: 'Muslim brotherhood & planet of the apes had a baby'. The ABC network immediately cancelled her popular show. Barr later blamed the tweet on her sleeping medication and called it a 'bad taste joke', which disavows the racism intrinsic to her tweet.

That the new racism coexists with and can so easily slip into hard biological conceptions of 'tiny brains' and 'apes' should alert us to the fact that it is easy to exaggerate the divide between an 'old' 'biological' and a 'new' 'cultural' racism. Monkey chants against black football players, or the throwing of banana skins at them, are other obvious illustrations.

Ambivalence and contradiction in racist and non-racist identities

It is interesting how often individuals who make racist comments blame the effects of alcohol or drugs in an attempt to explain away their racism. Roseanne Barr blamed her 'planet of the apes' tweet on her sleeping medication. The actor Mel Gibson, who shouted 'The Jews are responsible for all the wars in the world' in 2006 when arrested for a drink-driving offence, tried to save his reputation by claiming he was 'loaded' (with drink), 'angry' (at being wrongly treated), and having a 'nervous breakdown'. In 2011 the fashion designer John Galliano, sitting at a bar in the Marais district of Paris, insulted a couple sitting nearby who reported that he shouted 'fucking ugly Jewish bitch' and 'fucking Asian bastard' at them. They reported that he made thirty anti-Jewish insults in the space of forty-five minutes, and another woman said he had made similar insults to her in the same bar. Galliano, in his defence, said that he could not remember the offence because of a 'triple addiction' to alcohol, sleeping tablets, and Valium. He was fined, ordered to pay costs, and sacked from his post as creative director of the fashion house Dior. He said he had resorted to alcohol and prescription drugs because of stress at work and 'panic attacks'.

Alcohol is well known to lower inhibition. So, what exactly is one to make of such outbursts? What do they tell us about whether these individuals are *really* racist underneath a veneer of liberal toleration in their personalities?

My view is that we must understand identities as riven with contradiction and ambivalence. The 'common sense' of Western liberal democracies contains contradictory sentiments and values. On the one hand, there is a valorization of equality (buttressed by the historical memory that 'they' abolished slavery, neatly sidestepping that they had been complicit in it to begin with and that slave revolts played an important role), the desirability of 'diversity' (this being a more recent liberal 'add-on' in the wake of coloured immigration and feeble attempts at 'multiculturalism'), and a positive attitude being cultivated by governments towards the rich cultural mix provided by multiethnicity. However, on the other hand, there is the presence of the banal nationalism which I remarked upon earlier, and which so easily slides into a racialized frame of reference. Therefore, there coexists with the framework of equal rights and equal citizenship a racialized framework in which ethnic minorities are represented negatively in the media, added to which is the everyday rhetoric of racism that is always present (referring to Asians as 'Pakis', for example), the publicity given to Holocaust deniers, especially over social media in the age of the Internet, and so forth.

There is also the widely dispersed 'common-sense' but erroneous view that ethnic minorities are getting more than their fair share of national resources, especially via welfare, and that they are therefore a drain on what rightfully belongs only to the white majority. This coexists with the contradictory view that 'they are taking our jobs' (in which case they are not a burden on the welfare state).

There has also been a concerted attack on so-called 'political correctness', which has attempted to introduce a more inclusive view of the nation and has condemned racist epithets such as 'yid' and 'Paki'. The attack on 'political correctness' then turns racism disingenuously into an issue about 'free speech'; condemning the insult of calling Asians 'Pakis' or a Jewish person a 'yid' is then countered by the argument that this is a politically motivated and unwarranted restriction on 'freedom of speech'. It attempts to turn liberalism on its head and use it against attempts to curb common-sense, everyday racism.

My view on the 'I was drunk/drugged' defence is that individuals in Western nation states absorb both egalitarian and racialized narratives, taking on varying elements to varying degrees. In certain contexts, one or other view gains prominence. Racist views often get expressed by those who also hold more liberal and egalitarian views when alcohol consumption has loosened inhibitions. Attitudes towards ethnic minorities are often contradictory and ambivalent: this is the only way in which one can understand the sorts of outbursts by Mel Gibson and John Galliano.

Ambivalence is as much a characteristic as simple racism in the view of those who could simply be dismissed as racist. The issue of white ambivalence towards African Americans is a key theme of social psychologist Paul Wachtel's excellent discussion in *Race in the Mind of America*. In the case of the UK, an exhaustive reanalysis by Magne Flemmen and Mike Savage of existing research on racism comes to similar conclusions and is discussed in Chapter 6.

Racism and ethnocentrism as only 'natural'

It is worth pointing to other rhetorical strategies that enable ethnic minorities to be cast as permanently outside of nation and race. One is the view that it is only 'natural' to prefer 'one's own kind'. As Jean Marie Le Pen, erstwhile leader of the French Front National, put it, 'I prefer my daughters to my nieces, and my nieces to my neighbours . . . all men are the same.' The argument is then extended, either implicitly or explicitly, to one's own nation, religion, and race. The argument is presented as just common sense and part of human nature. Thus, racism can be 'naturalized', fusing biological and cultural ideas. This type of rhetorical move shifts the meaning of nation by likening the nation to a family, which of course is both a biological and cultural notion.

Another way of accomplishing this kind of exclusionary idea of the nation, and thus positioning certain types of immigrants as always outside the nation-race is the oft-expressed view that it is only human nature to protect one's own territory. Territory, nation, and race are thus naturalized. Enoch Powell, as usual, put it rather well in 1969: 'An instinct to preserve an identity and defend a territory is one of the deepest and strongest implanted in mankind.' The argument reappears in the discourse of 'national populists' and their apologists, as we shall see in Chapter 7.

For the present, note three consequences of such arguments. First, the argument from any type of *group* identity is conflated with the idea that *ethnic groups* and *nations* are *natural* entities that humans will instinctively defend. Second, it implies that *national* and ethnic animosities and hostility towards foreigners are only *natural*, and third, that immigrants or ethnic groups should only move to countries or neighbourhoods to which they can belong 'naturally'.

In effect the argument becomes one that says the 'natural' home of black and Asian immigrants cannot possibly be a white nation state such as Britain, France, or the Netherlands. This chain of reasoning ends up with the conclusion that it is unfair on both non-white immigrants and the white indigenous population that blacks and Asians should settle in these nation states. It is contrary to 'nature'.

Hence biology re-enters the cultural arena to bolster what then becomes an unambiguously racist argument that it is contrary to *nature* to think that white, black, and Asian populations could ever live harmoniously.

These types of arguments are based on selective and simplistic narratives that marginalize internal divisions within families as well as nations, and allow the family as a biological entity to function as a surrogate for nation, 'race', and whiteness.

Is 'cultural racism' racist?

If a purely cultural or religious argument devoid of any reference to biological relations is made, can it be called 'racist' without stretching the meaning of the label to a point where it becomes too wide to be useful as anything but a rhetorical ploy?

In principle, a form of group identification or classification that relies only on criteria such as mode of dress, language, customs, and religion, to name but a few, might more properly be subsumed under the ideas of *ethnicism* or *ethnocentrism* rather than having any connotations of 'race', and may be said to border on *xenophobia* if the criteria include membership of national groups and contain elements of hostility to 'foreigners' and non-nationals.

In practice, though, *cultural* demarcations are often drawn and used in a form that *naturalizes* them by implying that they are more or less *immutable*. Thus, the supposed avariciousness of

Jews, the alleged aggressiveness of Africans and African Americans, the criminality of Afro-Caribbeans, or the slyness of 'Orientals', become traits that are invariably attached to these groups over extremely long periods of time. The descriptions may then be drawn upon as part of a common-sense vocabulary of stereotypes that blurs any strict distinction between culture and biology.

Thus, the slippage into the idea of Jews as a 'race' *and* religious group is easily made via the bridging concept of an almost invariable trait of monetary greed, where the exception 'only proves the rule', thus making the statement immune to empirical counter-cases.

The argument I am making about the way social features are naturalized may be put in more technical social scientific terms by referring again to the concept of *essentialism*. That is, what allows cultural traits and biological classifications to operate together as part of an almost seamless framework is the notion of an unchanging 'essence' that underlies the superficial differences of historical time and place.

In *this* sense it is possible to talk of 'cultural racism' despite the fact that, strictly speaking, modern ideas of race have always had one or other biological foundation. To argue, as many do, that there has to be an explicit reference to biological features such as shape of nose, skin colour, or genetic inheritance if a proposition is to be described as racist is, strictly speaking, accurate. But it misses the point that generalizations, stereotypes, and other forms of cultural essentialism—the attribution of an unchanging essence to forms of thinking and acting, especially among ethnic groups— rest and draw upon a wider reservoir of concepts that are in circulation in popular and public culture. Thus, the racist elements of any particular proposition can only be judged by understanding the general context of public and private discourses in which ethnicity, national identifications, and race coexist in blurred and overlapping forms without clear demarcations.

This type of analysis is particularly relevant to the debates about whether hostility to Islam and Muslims, increasingly referred to as Islamophobia, is racist.

'Islamophobia' and cultural racism

Earlier, I demonstrated that racial classifications have from the outset included both cultural and biological elements.

Cultures, however, and the customs, beliefs, and behaviours that are encompassed by the term, obviously vary historically and geographically. Hence the usefulness of the concept of racialization, which sees racism as a *process*—as always a work in progress, so to speak—so that different elements are brought into play against the same groups in different times and places. Moreover, cultural racisms, which scrupulously attempt to eschew reference to biological markers, can be seen to include biological markers by implication and inference rather than directly. They *racialize* without 'race': Thatcher's remarks about 'New Commonwealth immigrants' is one such example.

Which brings us to hostility towards Islam and Muslims, which is now grouped under the umbrella term 'Islamophobia'—especially after a 1997 report by the UK-based Runnymede Trust on the subject put the term into wider circulation. By now, as Klug remarked in the journal *Ethnicities* in 2012, the concept has 'come of age'.

But can discrimination and hostility on the grounds of *religion* be regarded as a form of racism? The issue has been widely discussed. Confusion in the Runnymede report did not help. In providing illustrations of Islamophobia, physical assaults against South Asians who happened to be Muslim were not sufficiently distinguished from Asians who were specifically targeted for their obvious Muslim identity, for example women wearing the headscarf (hijab) or the face veil (niqab).

It thus fed into a current of opinion which argued that the report greatly exaggerated the degree of hostility to and discrimination against Muslims. It also enabled the criticism that the report's findings showed that what was at issue was a wider problem of racism: hostility towards Islam or Muslims was not the issue, or so the argument went.

Halliday, in a widely discussed critique, argued that animosity towards *Islam* was a historical and now less relevant phenomenon than hostility to *Muslims* as a people. However, critical responses to Halliday's argument soon pointed out that Islam can hardly be separated from Muslims, the people who practised the religion. The two are inseparable.

Some have argued that current Islamophobia has its historical roots in the military conflicts that occurred in early modern Europe, especially with the Crusades and the subsequent defeat of Islamic power in Spain in 1492. The use of the term 'crusade' by President George Bush in launching his 'war on terror' after the attack on the Twin Towers on 11 September 2001 has given credence to this view. But it is a mistake to use wide historical generalizations that underplay historical and geographical specificities.

More relevant is the 'Orientalism' that Said (1978) identified as the 'cultural imaginary' and mode of governance of Muslim lands by Western imperial powers, especially from the 19th century onwards. The 'Orient', in this set of processes, was homogenized, and its 'essence' regarded as immutable. The widely influential 'Clash of Civilizations' thesis advanced by the American political scientist Samuel P. Huntington in 1997 is testament to the enduring frame of the forever-continuing 'West versus Islam' (and other cultures) idea that Said had highlighted.

In similar racialized tropes, there are the conspiracy theories that argue there is a plot by Muslims to take over Europe, by demographic expansion by Muslims within Europe, the expansion of mosque building, the development of sharia law as a parallel system, and the conversion of Christians to Islam. The theories posit a singular, homogenized Judaeo-Christian Europe that is under threat by a correspondingly homogenous Islam and Muslim population (which continues to ignore the diverse ethnicities and national origins of Muslims), while a taken-for-granted assumption of European 'whiteness' flies below the radar of the notion of religious conflict, racializing it even further.

This then makes the 'fear of Islam' rational. It has been nurtured, in France for example, by hateful remarks by members of the French assembly and even government ministers, and a constant stream of cartoons in the magazine *Charlie Hebdo* (with a notorious, lethal, and completely unacceptable backlash against the journalists who worked for it). In addition, the fear of Islam and Muslims is fed by the misogyny that is deeply institutionalized in many Muslim-majority countries. 'Islam' is then homogenized as a backward, anti-modern culture barely admissible within the ambit of 'civilization'. Ignored are the secular regimes and processes that have historically been evident in many Muslim-majority countries such as Egypt, Turkey, Morocco, and Tunisia, as well as the secularism evident in second- and third-generation migrants from these countries. This complex set of ideas and attacks begins to make the ideas of those who might be labelled 'Islamophobes' irrefutable. Added to this is the fact that French Muslims are often targeted in 'hate' crimes. In June 2018 a right-wing plot to kill veiled women and imams, and destroy grocery shops selling halal meat, mosques, and Muslim community centres was thwarted by French authorities.

The debates have now become too wide ranging and the literature too voluminous to be considered in any depth here. It is thus appropriate to return to the issue that is most germane to the subject matter of this book: can anti-Islamic and anti-Muslim hostility be regarded as a form of racism? If it is acknowledged, rightly, that racism always combines cultural and biological features, anti-Islam and anti-Muslim sentiments appear to satisfy the cultural element, for religion is indeed a cultural phenomenon. I have also suggested how, within the notion of a Judaeo-Christian Europe, some or other idea of 'whiteness' is inferentially smuggled in.

But there are black Muslims and white Muslims, as well as Asian Muslims and Arab Muslims; Muslims are constituted by a wide variety of nationalities and ethnicities, while the religion itself is riven with sectarian conflict, especially between Shi'as and Sunnis. *Muslims, in other words, cannot be considered a 'race'.*

However, this is by no means an argument that prevents us from recognizing the myriad ways in which Muslims are *racialized*. In particular, the notion that there are specific visual markers that can be used to identify followers of Islam enable Muslims to be racialized. The beard for men, and the headscarf and veil for women, become racializing markers, especially as this is usually conflated with the Muslim body as non-white. Cartoons of the prophet Muhammad habitually portray him as stereotypically having a hooked, 'Arabic-Semitic' nose and brown skin. This combines with the constant refrain from many in Europe and the USA that Muslims are intrinsically culturally inassimilable, thus essentializing and *naturalizing* Islam and Muslims. Constant complaints that Muslim communities are not 'integrating' properly into Western values and ways of life shade into the idea that they are permanently 'outsiders' in relation to the West. Again, the huge variation in the secularization and 'Westernization' among younger generations of Muslims is simply swept away.

Research studies, for example by Sian and Sayyid, and Carr, reveal a large number of cases in which Muslims seeking employment are told that their appearance, clothing, and religious customs have been a barrier. Research studies in which Muslims submit two identical CVs, one with a Muslim name and the other with a Christian name, have found that their chances of being called for interview improve dramatically when Christian names are used. The British government, in an attempt to recruit universities to spy on their Muslim students, were told to look out for 'Asian looking' students who showed signs of radicalization, as was reported in the *Guardian* newspaper on 16 October 2006. There is a case for the argument that Muslims, while not a 'race', are definitely racialized in the UK, in the rest of Europe, and in the USA. Take just one more illustration for the time being: the *Guardian* newspaper's investigation into racial bias in housing in the UK, published on 4 December 2018, revealed that a person with a Muslim name looking for a room to rent received significantly fewer positive responses than one who called himself 'David'.

Stereotyping in the British mass media, especially tabloid newspapers, plays an important role, as in all forms of racialization. Research by many, including Morey and Yakin, shows how Muslim representation is trapped within a narrow range of stereotypes. One feature common to stereotyping, and which also applies to Muslims, is the splitting of the 'good Muslim' from the 'bad Muslim', but with no category in between. How then is one to characterize the moderate, law-abiding, but scrupulous Muslim who attends mosque for prayers, or the moderate Muslim woman who wears a headscarf? If they are vehemently opposed to violence, but are critical of Western policies in the Middle East, are they 'good' or 'bad' Muslims? The very wide net of 'Islamist' catches a large proportion of Muslims in a double bind from which it is impossible to escape without jettisoning all critical interpretations, which are shared by a large number of non-Muslims, that the Western invasions of Iraq and Afghanistan have been disastrous and undertaken under false pretences—for example linking Saddam Hussein to Al-Qaeda—and that the invasion of Iraq was very possibly illegal.

Perhaps the most important point in this debate has been missing from all the accounts considered so far. It is David Tyrer, in his book *The Politics of Islamophobia*, who has made the obvious but powerful argument that the populations being discussed as 'Muslims' were *already racialized* as 'Pakis' and 'Arabs'. So the point about whether Muslims are a race or not is somewhat beside the point. 'Muslims' have only appeared in the frame of 'race' after they had already put in an appearance in the framework of racialization, but under another guise, before they themselves began to assert the Islamic aspect of their identities, a phenomenon that occurred in the wake of the 1979 Iranian revolution and the Salman Rushdie affair over his book *The Satanic Verses*.

The racializing of Muslims as Muslims simply adds another racializing layer to an already racialized population. If anything, Muslims are doubly racialized, first as 'Pakis', 'Asians', 'Arabs', 'Moroccans', 'Turks', and other descriptions ('goat fuckers' being one of them, as applied to Arabs), and then also as bearded, skull cap, hijab, and burqa wearing, non-white heathens who have, in cultural and biological terms, made their home in white, Judaeo-Christian nations to which they do not naturally belong and pose an existential threat. As the German footballer of Turkish heritage, Mesut Özil, who resigned from the German national team in 2018, put it, 'I am German when we win, but an immigrant when we lose'. 'Immigrant', of course, is another racialized epithet which is deployed to cast individuals and populations as permanently outside the nation, and is indiscriminately applied to people of South Asian, Somali, and Arab origin.

These double and treble racializations are then, as with other forms of racialization, also sexualized. In the UK, this has been a process enhanced by the tabloid and other mass media treatment of groups of men of Pakistani and other Muslim heritage who have groomed young white girls for sex and sex trafficking. The fact that much grooming is carried out by white men is never mentioned, making it possible to argue that it is something about their religion that makes these Asian men prone to such behaviour. As many researchers have pointed out, the involvement of these Asian men has little to do with their religion and mostly to do with their involvement in the night-time trade of taxis and takeaways, to which vulnerable young women, both white and Muslim, gravitate.

When all these processes of racialization are factored in there can be little doubt that 'Islamophobia' names a form of labelling that carries strong racial connotations and needs to be considered as part of the racial politics of not only the UK, but the rest of Europe and the USA.

The 'new antisemitism'

Perhaps more than that of any other people, the history of the Jewish people has been characterized by a deep, longstanding hostility, persecution, and even genocide. Much of the early persecution of Jews was by Christians. Jews were reviled in very early times as the murderers of Christ. An even more virulent anti-Judaism is evident from the 12th century onwards, including the notorious 'Blood Libel' (the belief that Jews used Christian blood, especially that of children, for matzos or unleavened bread, at Passover). The Crusades against Muslim powers in Europe also led to massacres of Jews in 1096. The final success of the Crusades in 1492 led not only to the expulsion of Muslims from Spain, but Jews as well, as noted earlier. The idea of Jews as a people obsessed with money, which preceded as well as followed this expulsion, was a result of measures that banned Jews from many occupations, confining them to moneylending and usury. Clergy and monarchs who craved a luxurious lifestyle not only made many Jews wealthy but led to indebtedness among churchmen and royalty. The latter, unable or unwilling to pay, often instigated violent persecutions which robbed Jews of their wealth.

It was perhaps inevitable that the 19th century, so preoccupied with the idea of 'race', would find a place for Jews in racial classifications. In the 1870s, as noted earlier, it was the German Wilhelm Marr who seems to have first claimed a scientific basis for regarding the Jews as a 'race'. With the rise of Nazism in the first half of the 20th century, this pseudo-scientific notion led, together with other causal drivers, to the greatest catastrophe suffered by Jews, six million of whom perished in the most brutal manner in the Holocaust.

The aftermath of World War II, in which the Nazi German state was comprehensively defeated, led to the formation of the United Nations, and as we saw earlier its cultural arm UNESCO issued a 'Statement on Race', which declared that there was no scientific basis for the idea of 'race', thus undercutting all foundations for discrimination based on 'race', including the persecution of Jews. The UNESCO statement led to a reformulation, especially in the social sciences, in which all racism was seen as stemming from unwarranted, irrational hostility and 'prejudice'. Gordon Allport's book *The Nature of Prejudice*, published in 1954, is the *locus classicus* for this type of perspective on racism.

Subsequently, although not without opposition from those with a vested interested in upholding their own power, a great many countries have enacted what is often called, especially in the UK, 'race relations' legislation, which makes it illegal to discriminate on grounds of 'race', a notion that has subsequently been expanded to include ethnicity, nationality, and, in some cases, religion.

However, it was only in May 2016 that the International Holocaust Remembrance Alliance (IHRA) issued what it referred to as a 'working definition' of antisemitism. The IHRA statements were a response to rising antisemitic verbal and physical abuse against Jews in Europe, and the growing numbers of those who denied that the Holocaust ever happened. Thus, the IHRA also adopted a 'Working Definition of Holocaust Denial and Distortion'.

The IHRA 'working definition' defines antisemitism in the following terms: 'Antisemitism is a certain perception of Jews, which may be expressed as hatred towards Jews. Rhetorical and physical manifestations of antisemitism are directed towards Jewish or non-Jewish individuals and/or property, towards Jewish community institutions and religious facilities.' This formulation is regarded by the IHRA as a 'non-legally binding' working definition. The draftees of the working definition acknowledged its somewhat loose and vague wording, and thus added a number of 'examples' 'which may serve as illustrations'.

Eleven examples are provided, at least six of which pertain to the state of Israel. This is not surprising, for many individual Jews and Jewish organizations feel that there is often a slippage in which criticisms of the state of Israel are not sufficiently and rigorously distinguished from criticisms of Jewish people. In other words, criticisms of the actions of the state of Israel and antisemitism are conflated in many statements and in actions taken against the state of Israel.

In essence, in the UK and to some degree in the USA, this is said to be the 'new antisemitism': criticisms of the state of Israel that do not discriminate sufficiently between Israel and Jewish people whether in Israel or outside Israel. It is often argued that the British left is the main perpetrator of this form of antisemitism. The concept of a new antisemitism in France, although sharing a similar history, also has a specific genealogy, which is discussed later in this section.

The failure of the Oslo peace accords between Israel and the Palestinians in the 1990s, which was then followed by an *intifada* or uprising by Palestinians, led to fierce debates about the actions of the state of Israel in its continued occupation and encouragement and protection of Jewish settlements in the Occupied Territories of the West Bank, and its treatment of Palestinian inhabitants. In international law these settlements are illegal, and have involved the absorption of territories that had been in the hands of Palestinians. It is not surprising, then, that the actions of the state of Israel have come under intense international scrutiny, especially as a great many Palestinians have been shot by Israeli troops. On the other hand, the Palestinians, especially the militant group Hamas and its supporters, have been guilty of firing missiles over the Israeli border from Gaza, the area under Hamas control.

Not all Israelis of Jewish descent support the actions of the state of Israel, nor do many Jewish people who do not reside in Israel. A rigorous distinction between Israel and Jewish people is obviously necessary if criticisms of the actions of the state of Israel are not to 'slip' into criticisms of all Jewish people, which would certainly be a form of antisemitism.

The working definition's examples thus suggest, as illustrations of antisemitism, statements which accuse Jewish citizens outside Israel of 'being more loyal to Israel, or to the alleged priorities of Jews worldwide'; 'denying Jewish people their right to self-determination e.g. by claiming that the existence of Israel is a racist endeavour'; 'applying double standards by requiring of it a behaviour not expected or demanded of other democratic nations'; 'drawing comparison of Israeli policies to that of Nazis'; 'holding Jews collectively responsible for actions of the state of Israel'.

At least thirty-one countries, including the UK, have adopted the definition and all the examples. In the UK at least 130 local councils, the Crown Prosecution Service, and the judiciary have adopted the definition and examples in full. In 2018 the British Labour Party found itself embroiled in controversy inside and outside the party when it attempted to amend the examples—not the working definition, it must be said—to ensure that legitimate criticism of Israel was not prevented by adopting the definition and all its examples. After lengthy debate the Labour Party has now accepted in full all the examples as well as the working definition.

Many commentators have argued that the British Labour Party's attempt to alter the examples was an example of 'antisemitism'. There is no doubt that many members of the Labour Party, during the debates and before, have made remarks that by any standards are antisemitic. At least two well-argued books, one by Hirsch and the other by Fine and Spencer, have made a convincing case that there are antisemitic elements within the left, and antisemitism has also been revealed by investigative journalists.

The controversy continues, now including what many argue are not well-founded claims that Israel is an 'apartheid' state, analogous to the notorious South African state that oppressed all non-whites within South Africa. In the limited space available in this book, it is not possible to discuss the extremely complex issues involved. Note, though, two features of recent discussions, on the Israeli as well the Palestinian side. The former Israeli Prime Minister Ehud Barak claimed in a German television interview in June 2017 that unless a two-state solution was implemented, Israel would find itself on a 'slippery slope to apartheid', for it would find itself 'controlling the whole area from the Mediterranean to the River Jordan where some 13 million people are living—eight million Israelis and five million Palestinians', but with only Israel reigning over this territory. Also, in the wake of legislation passed by the Israeli Knesset in July 2018 stating that

Jews have a unique right to self-determination and demoting Arabic to a secondary status, thus making Arabs second-class citizens, the world-renowned Israeli musician and conductor Daniel Barenboim argued that the law was 'racist' and made him ashamed to be an Israeli. Barenboim stated, 'It follows that [this law] is clearly a form of apartheid'.

Of course, this is not the definitive view on the matter, but when a person of his stature and commitment to Jewish self-determination states a view of this type, it is time to reflect on the course upon which the Israeli state seems to be set.

On the other hand, it is equally important to take note of the antisemitic remarks of the current Palestinian President Mahmoud Abbas, who declared in May 2018 that the root cause of the Holocaust was not so much the Nazis' genocidal hatred of Jews, but the behaviour of the Jews themselves, especially their 'social behaviour', adding that he meant 'their social function related to banks and interest'. This is simply old antisemitism, repeating an age-old stereotype. It demonstrates that the new antisemitism seems to be often underpinned by a very old form of prejudice and hostility to Jewish people. Note, though, that the same Ehud Barak who warned of the dangers of Israeli apartheid, said in a May 2002 interview (reported in the *Guardian* on 23 May 2002) that 'Arabs don't suffer from the problem of telling lies that exists in Judaeo-Christian culture', thus neatly combining race, geography, religion, and culture in a formulation that not only captures the common-sense racism that is widespread, but bedevils and poisons relations between Palestinians and Israelis in particular, putting huge hurdles in the way of any path to peace.

While many of these factors have influenced events that have also been labelled a new antisemitism in France, the context is different. Charges of a new antisemitism in the UK, and to some extent in the USA, have been primarily levelled at the left, especially now that extreme right-wing groups have focused their

hate on Muslims rather than Jews in an attempt to distance
themselves from antisemitism. In France it is Muslims, of North
and West African origin, whose members are generally regarded
as part of *minorités visibles*, or visible minorities, who are said to
be the perpetrators of the new antisemitism. The term is deployed
to distinguish it from an 'old', longstanding Catholic antisemitism.
Whites, being the majority of the population, do not enter the
frame of this racialized discourse, but of course this is because the
'white gaze' is the norm underlying French universalism and
therefore has an 'invisible', taken-for-granted, 'universalist'
presence which defines who must be regarded as being out of
place but in full *sight*, as outsiders in the national culture.

The French left, not unlike the British and American left, is
accused by Jewish and other intellectuals of downplaying the new
antisemitism in what is regarded as a misguided attempt to
prevent the demonization of all French Muslims who have been
the target of hateful invective in French public discourse.

Matters came to a head in 2017 and 2018 when two elderly Jewish
women were murdered by Muslim men. On 28 March 2018 a
large march was organized by Jewish organizations and was
attended by a large number of Muslims. Soon an open letter
signed by 250 well-known French people, including one former
president, asked French Muslims to publicly proclaim their
support for the French Republic, but also argued that some
paragraphs of the Qur'an should be excised, provoking a response
from Muslim imams denouncing antisemitism and what they saw
as the Islamophobia that they identified in the letter.

Anglo-American new antisemitism differs from the French
version, which some label 'postcolonial antisemitism'. During the
colonial period, French colonial authorities gave full French
citizenship to Algerian Jews, but not to Arab Muslims, and after
Algerian independence Jews entered France as full citizens while
Muslims had to apply for citizenship. Moreover, it is well known

in France that there is a strong resentment among French Muslims that while the Holocaust is publicly remembered, for example in black plaques on every building in Paris from which a Jewish child was deported by the wartime Vichy government to almost certain death, the sins of slavery are given short shrift. While Paris has a major Holocaust museum and research centre, the only museum that documents the history of France's role in the slave trade is in Guadeloupe, an overseas French territory some 7,000 km from the French mainland.

But French new antisemitism has also become intertwined with far-right infiltration into protests by the 'yellow vests' (*gilets jaunes*), which initially began as protests against fuel price rises but have morphed into wider antagonisms against falling living standards and elitism.

While discussing the new antisemitism, it is important to remember that the tropes of the 'old', conventional antisemitism abound. To take just one prominent example, George Soros, the Jewish Hungarian-born financier and philanthropist, is consistently accused by right-wingers of financing a conspiracy against the West. It has been reported that the British politician Nigel Farage claimed that Soros wants to fundamentally reshape Europe's racial make-up and to end the continent's Christian culture, and that Soros is 'the biggest danger to the entire Western world', as reported by the UK *Guardian* newspaper on 12 May 2019. The Hungarian prime minister, Viktor Orbán, has consistently shown antisemitic hostility towards Soros; so much so that Soros has been forced to move his Central European University, originally based in Budapest, to Vienna. Only small parts of the university will be based in Budapest in the future.

The survival and indeed prominence of the old, classic tropes of antisemitism have been given a further prominence with the rise of right-wing national populism in Europe, a phenomenon discussed in Chapter 7.

Chapter 5
Structural racism and colourblind whiteness

Structural and systemic racism

From a sociological perspective, current racialized inequalities in white-dominated societies in North America and Europe need to be explored in systemic, structural terms. That is, while individual 'prejudice' against populations regarded as non-white, or 'ethnic minorities' including white ethnic minorities, is obviously significant—social structures, after all, always involve actors, actions, motives, and conscious and unconscious practices—to understand how racialized inequalities persist over time it becomes necessary to understand how there exist networks of social relations and institutions which have the effect of sustaining a combination of actions, cultures, and practices which then reproduce racialized inequalities over time.

It is important to acknowledge that these structures of racialized inequalities are not unchanging. Individuals from previously subordinate racialized minorities can and do move up the socio-economic hierarchy, such that black people in the USA, for example, now have a substantial middle class composed of businesspeople, lawyers, doctors, school teachers, and academics teaching and researching at university level. It is also the case that both in the USA and the UK, for example, over time fewer and fewer individuals will explicitly identify as 'racist' or 'racially prejudiced'. For a lengthy period since the arrival of so-called 'coloured immigrants' into the UK after the end of World War II, the numbers of those claiming to be racially prejudiced have been falling. For example, unlike the very racially hostile period that characterized public life during the 1950s and 1960s, research in 2017 by the British National Centre for Research, in collaboration with the Runnymede Trust, found that 26 per cent of people described themselves as 'very' or a 'little' prejudiced towards people of other 'races'.

However, this figure has risen from when a similar survey was undertaken in 2001. It has been argued that growing hostility may be explained by rising intolerance towards Muslims since the attacks of 9/11. Note, though, that in 1987 38 per cent of people polled said that they were either 'very or a little prejudiced' against people of other 'races'.

Results from this type of survey research need to be interpreted with caution, because respondents have become only too aware that 'racial prejudice' is frowned upon, partly as a result of race relations legislation that has outlawed direct and indirect discrimination.

Structural or systemic racism cannot be treated completely separately from what has come to be called 'institutional racism'. Societies are made up of institutions such as schools, prisons, the courts that administer justice, hospitals, and police forces. Systemic or structural racism is usually applied as a concept to characterize a set of interrelated relationships that include institutions and individuals. Studies of structural and systemic racism therefore focus on how the interrelationships reproduce the subordinate and superior positions occupied by racialized populations. White people, of course, are included as part of racialized groups, for they occupy a dominant position in the USA and the UK, which are societies that are in general racialized. A distinction has to be made between 'whiteness' and white people in the context of structural racism, and any discussion of whites has to be recognized as also racialized. It is important to grasp that a focus on 'whiteness' is not to make the absurd claim that all white people are racist, an issue that has also bedevilled discussions of institutional racism.

It is my view, also expressed earlier, that it is necessary to reject the view that it is easy to differentiate, in any definitive manner, racists from non-racists. Such an exercise is likely to be exceptionally difficult, misleading, and unproductive, although it is necessary to accept at face value the proclaimed racism of far-right and neo-Nazi activists. Racialized identities, as I argued earlier, are riven with ambivalence and contradiction. Diagnosing racism is not a clinical practice akin to that undertaken in medicine. White people are racialized, for they live in societies where processes and structures of racialization exist, not necessarily because they are individually racist.

Institutional racism

The idea of institutional racism goes back to the late 1960s in the USA, when Stokely Carmichael and Charles V. Hamilton used it in *Black Power* (1967), their powerful indictment of persistent black inequalities. Carmichael and Hamilton wanted to highlight the process whereby, no matter whether the individual motivations and behaviour of ordinary white people were racist or not, all whites benefited from social structures and organizational patterns that continually disadvantaged blacks, while allowing whites to stay well ahead in living standards, including housing, health and life span, neighbourhood amenities and safety, educational facilities and achievement, level of employment, and income and wealth.

They made it clear that this process could never be completely impersonal and unintentional. 'Institutional racism', they argued, 'relies on the active and pervasive operation of anti-black attitudes and practices. A sense of superior group position prevails: whites are "better" than blacks...This is a racist attitude and it permeates the society, on both the individual and institutional level, covertly and overtly.'

Institutional racism was used to highlight the fact that the playing field in which blacks and whites competed for decent standards of living was not level. It was *systematically* skewed against blacks, both in terms of opportunities and outcomes. A vicious circle gripped black lives. A version of this view was endorsed in the 1968 Kerner Commission's report into black neighbourhood uprisings in the USA.

However, the concept has found more fertile ground in the UK than the USA. Sir William Macpherson's inquiry into the murder in south London of black teenager Stephen Lawrence, and the subsequent police investigation, focused public attention on institutional racism by claiming that in part at least it was to blame for the failure of the police operation to find the murderers. In his 1999 report institutional racism was defined as 'the collective failure of an organization to provide an appropriate and professional service to people because of their colour, culture or ethnic origin. It can be seen or detected in processes, attitudes and behaviour which amount to discrimination through unwitting prejudice, ignorance, thoughtlessness, and racist stereotyping which disadvantage minority ethnic people.'

This is not that far removed from the original definition of Carmichael and Hamilton, and as Karim Murji has pointed out, shows a remarkable set of transitions from usage by political activists, then into sociology and subsequently into mainstream public political debate. The concept is not without its limitations. It is not difficult for representatives of institutions such as police forces to argue—as indeed they did in response to the Macpherson Report—that the public perception of being branded 'institutionally racist' will tar all individuals within it as 'racist'.

Also, encounters between police and young black and Asian men are not solely defined by racialization; they become contests of masculinity. Racialization is interwoven with other forms of identity, as we shall see in the discussion of 'intersectionality'.

This is why I have suggested, in an essay on the uses of the concept of racialization, that the concept of *institutional racialization* is more appropriate. It denotes both that 'race' is not the only factor at play in institutional practices, for class and gender may also be involved, and that any large institution, whether the police force or the BBC (which has been described as being 'hideously white' by its former director-general, Greg Dyke, although he stopped short of calling the BBC institutionally racist, which is how it was often interpreted at the time), is likely to contain departments with varying degrees of witting and unwitting racism. Both Murji and Professor Steve Garner have agreed with my suggestion that institutional racialization is a fruitful concept with which to analyse institutions, rather than the more static and blunt notion of institutional racism with which to brand whole institutions such as the police force.

Moreover, it has become obvious that despite the emphasis by Macpherson and others on issues of *unwitting* prejudice, and thus the need for subtle but searching programmes of anti-racist education, there is a tendency for charges of institutional racism to result more in bureaucratic initiatives for ethnic monitoring (racial profiling as it is called in the USA) and greater ethnic minority recruitment, rather than a change in racist stereotyping and racist culture in the police force. Post-Macpherson, in 2019 Leroy Logan, a former Metropolitan Police officer and ex-chairman of the National Black Police Association, claimed, twenty years after the Macpherson Report, that the Metropolitan Police is still institutionally racist, especially in the manner in which it treats black police officers and black members of the public. In 2015 the Metropolitan Police commissioner, Sir Bernard Hogan-Howe, admitted that there was some justification in regarding the Metropolitan Police as still institutionally racist, and claimed that (British) 'society is institutionally racist', judging by the under-representation of ethnic minorities 'from judges to doctors, to journalists, to editors, to governments'.

In many respects, in the USA little has changed since the Kerner Report of 1968 expressed concern that 'our nation is moving towards two societies, one black, one white—separate and unequal'. Later studies by Hacker, Massey, and Denton, and by Brown and colleagues, among others, show how institutional racism continues to blight black lives, but also those of people of Hispanic origin. Inadequate housing (the product of years of discrimination and 'white flight') and poorly resourced schools lead to low educational achievement, lower admissions to colleges, and poor employment prospects. All of these are exacerbated by persistent hostility from white employers. The result is a cycle of high unemployment, drug taking, crime, and unsafe neighbourhoods. Biased policing and courts, and poor legal resources, mean proportionately more arrests and convictions, and longer sentences. Black children thus grow up in an environment that systematically undermines their aspirations and leads to massive underachievement. The result is that black communities, especially, remain at the bottom of the American pile generation after generation.

Recent findings confirm the relative stability of wealth and income disparities of the earlier research cited above. Less than half of black families (41 per cent) and Hispanic families (45 per cent) live in owner-occupied housing, compared to white families for whom the figure is 71 per cent. Median earnings for black males are 32 per cent lower than median earnings for whites. The earnings gap between white and Hispanic men grew from 29 per cent to 42 per cent between 1970 and 2010. In 2013, a white family's median wealth was $141,900. For every dollar of wealth owned by whites, the median African American family had less than 8 cents in wealth, and the median Hispanic family had less than 10 cents. Other research, for example the Pew Research Center's analysis of government data, suggests that the median wealth of white households is twenty times that of black households and eighteen times that of Hispanic households.

The mortgage crisis that began in 2007–8 from the sale of subprime mortgages impacted more on black and Hispanic families, for they were disproportionately targeted by predatory mortgage lenders, and so too did the credit 'crunch' that followed. Homeownership, of course, is the most important means for American (and British) families to accumulate wealth. While the foreclosure rate for white families caught up in the subprime crisis was 5 per cent, it was nearly double that for African Americans, and for Hispanics it was 11.9 per cent. The fall in house prices meant that 31 per cent of families of colour owed more than their houses were worth. The loss of wealth among American communities showed wide disparities: although the average loss to all families, including white families, was 28.5 per cent between 2005 and 2009, Asian Americans lost 54 per cent and black families lost 47.6 per cent of their wealth. In 2011, the Bank of America agreed to pay $335 million to settle a federal government claim that its mortgage division, Countrywide Financial, discriminated against black and Hispanic homebuyers, although the bank continued to deny the allegations.

In 2017, African American workers had the highest unemployment rate, at 7.5 per cent, while the figure for Hispanics was 4.9 per cent. White workers had the lowest unemployment rate, at 3.5 per cent.

Some of the most dramatic statistics concern the rates of incarceration of the American black population. In 2014 African Americans constituted 34 per cent, or 2.3 million, of the total incarcerated population of 6.8 million. Though African Americans and Hispanics together make up some 32 per cent of the US population, they constituted 56 per cent of all incarcerated

American people in 2015. African Americans are incarcerated at more than five times the rate of whites. If African Americans and Hispanics were incarcerated at the same rate as whites, the prison population of the USA would decline by almost 40 per cent. Research shows that African Americans and whites use drugs at similar rates (in fact some studies show that drug use is lower among African Americans), but the imprisonment rate of African Americans is almost six times that of whites, largely due to what in the USA is called 'racial profiling' in policing, so that African Americans are more heavily policed and suffer more from stop and search, especially for minor traffic offences—a fact that has given rise to the wry comment that 'driving while black' has itself become an offence. In some states, black men have been imprisoned on drug charges at rates that vary between twenty and fifty times those of white men. In turn, a criminal record has a negative impact that is twice as large for African American applicants as it is for whites.

Much of this is documented in Michelle Alexander's book *The New Jim Crow*, which shows in great detail the ways in which African Americans find themselves disadvantaged at all stages of the criminal justice system. Moreover, criminalization has severe disadvantaging effects not only in employment, but in housing, education, public benefits, and, in many states, voting rights, because convicted felons are not allowed to vote. Her analysis leads her to conclude that the escalation of the so-called 'war on drugs' during the Reagan era of the 1980s has had particularly lasting effects, with the African American prison population expanding from 300,000 in the 1980s to more than two million today. This, she argues, should be seen for what it is—'mass incarceration'—and that it has resulted from a backlash against the gains made in the civil rights struggles by African Americans from the 1960s onwards. The fact that the criminal justice system operates as part of an *institutional* complex of *structural* racism rather than simply individual prejudice is attested to by the documentation provided by James Forman Jr that large numbers of African Americans are involved in the law-enforcement process, including black mayors, judges, and police officers, all of whom got caught up in the federal 'war on drugs' which impacted on the poorest blacks who lived in conditions that generated violence.

Of course, racism plays its part. For example, the following disparities suggest that racism affects what happens to blacks in the criminal justice system: black defendants are more likely to be sentenced to execution than white defendants, and those who commit crimes against black victims are less harshly punished than those whose victims are white.

Post-imperial panics: ethnic segregation and 'race riots' in 21st-century Britain

British race relations legislation has often been held up as a model for the rest of the European Union. Yet, nearly thirty years after the seminal 1976 Act, which added indirect discrimination as unlawful, Trevor Phillips, chair of the Commission for Racial Equality, was warning the country that it was in danger of 'sleepwalking' into 'segregation'. How had Britain, with its self-image of a liberal, tolerant, and fair-minded nation, and its official adoption of multiculturalism, come to be on the verge of what was described by many as 'a US-type nightmare'?

The official inquiries into the 2001 disorders by mainly British Asian youth in former textile mill towns and cities in northern England did indeed paint a picture of white and Asian communities increasingly separated in patterns of residence, schooling, friendship, and employment.

Moreover, the reports into the disorders in the northern cities pointed out that the areas involved were among the poorest 20 per cent in the country, and some of the more specific urban wards where the South Asian and white populations involved lived were actually in the poorest 1 per cent of the whole country.

In 2011 there were further 'race riots', mostly although not solely involving black youth, after the police shooting of a black man in the Tottenham area of London. The same area had seen violent disorders thirty years previously on the Blackwater Farm estate after the death of a British woman of African Caribbean origin in a police raid on her home.

Racial discrimination and ethnic inequalities in Britain

In the aftermath of the end of World War II, Britain suffered acute labour shortages, especially in lower-skilled and unskilled occupations. Positions, for example, in the textiles, car, and other manufacturing industries, transport, and the newly formed NHS were filled by migrants from Britain's former colonies of the Indian subcontinent (subdivided into India and Pakistan, and subsequently Bangladesh after it broke away from Pakistan) and the islands of the Caribbean, especially Jamaica and Barbados. British Transport and the NHS were particularly proactive in the recruitment of bus conductors and nurses, for example.

Blatant racial discrimination by employers and landlords, widely documented in numerous research reports, led, in part, to the formation of marginalized black and Asian communities in deprived areas in London, Birmingham, Manchester, and a great many towns in the north of England. Successive governments, although economically reliant on 'coloured' workers, remained anxious about the new arrivals and for many years did nothing to prevent discrimination that was openly on display in the windows in houses, for example, which baldly stated: 'No coloureds, no dogs', sometimes adding 'no Irish' as well.

The patterns of immigration and discrimination that characterized the post-war period led, not surprisingly, to a distinct and disadvantaged place for Britain's growing 'coloured' minority.

The latest studies as of October 2018 reveal, among other things, the following disparities between whites and ethnic minorities, including those classified as 'mixed', whether between Asian and white or black and white.

The unemployment rate for black, Asian, and minority ethnic (BAME) people, at 8 per cent, is twice as high as for whites. People of Pakistani and Bangladeshi origin are more likely to be confined to low-skilled, low-paying occupations (this is a systemic reproduction of their original insertion into the British occupational structure). BAME households tend to suffer from higher rates of poor-quality housing and spend a higher proportion of their income on housing. Of all households, black people are least likely to own their own homes, while those of Bangladeshi origin are most likely to suffer from overcrowding. Around 40 per cent of people from ethnic minorities live in low-income households, which is twice the rate as that for white people. Within minorities there is wide variation, with 60 per cent of Pakistani-origin and 70 per cent of Bangladeshi-origin people living in low-income households; the comparative figure for whites is 20 per cent and for black Caribbean people and for Indians 30 per cent. Black men are six times more likely to be stopped and searched by police than white men. Black women are most likely to experience anxiety and depression while black men are most likely to have suffered from a psychotic disorder. Black Caribbean pupils were permanently excluded from schooling at three times the rate of white pupils.

BAME groups have shown recent increases in entry into higher education, with slightly more than a fifth now in higher education. But BAME students are least likely to be studying at the more prestigious Russell Group universities, are more likely to get lower-class degrees, and are less likely to be employed six months after graduating.

Some Asian pupils, especially those of Indian and Chinese origin, have been performing better than white pupils. And Indian-origin people are the most likely of all ethnic minority groups to be in the highest-skilled occupations and the professions, but they are underrepresented at senior levels both in the public and private sectors. A 2018 study published in the *BMJ* shows that black and Asian doctors earn less on average than their white colleagues, and ethnic minority consultants in the NHS earn less than their white counterparts.

The inequalities documented here are of a structural, systemic, and institutional type. They relate to outcomes, without documenting that they are the product of conscious, 'witting' discrimination, although outcomes depend not only on embedded background socio-economic conditions but also on individual or collective acts of overt discrimination. The existence of the latter coexist with a taken-for-granted preference for 'people like us', which of course also discriminates against white working-class-origin people in the labour market.

However, there is also general agreement among researchers that some ethnic minority groups in particular have made improvements to their relative position since the 1980s. As we have seen, these are primarily people of Indian, African Asian (mostly Indians from East and Central Africa), and Chinese origin.

Ethnic segregation in general is not near American levels, although it is undoubtedly the case that in some northern cities, such as Bradford, Burnley, and Oldham, where young South Asians, white youth, and police clashed in 2001, white and non-white communities live largely 'parallel' lives, with separate residential areas and schools and very little intercommunal socializing. It has been well documented that this is partly due to 'white flight', with white residents moving out very soon after South Asians either begin to move into rental properties or buy houses in such areas. Another reason, of course, is that ethnic minorities themselves buy or rent in areas where their own communities of origin have begun to settle, to access community support and facilities such as places of worship or shops that sell foodstuffs that are part of their diet. However, all studies show that ethnic minorities would rather live in ethnically mixed areas, and express regret that white residents have moved out. This is especially true of the second and third generations of those descended from the original migrants.

It thus becomes necessary to explore in greater depth the meanings of 'whiteness'.

Seeing but not being seen: the fact of whiteness

On the afternoon of 25 February 2015, the BBC broadcast an episode of its regular and popular radio programme, *Thinking Allowed*, which is presented by a well-known retired sociologist and public commentator, Professor Laurie Taylor. The programme, among other things, involved a trip to Cape Town, South Africa, and Taylor narrated the following events. He had visited a middle-class suburb of the city and had walked undisturbed to his destination. The following day, he went down the same street, but accompanied by another man. Suddenly the street was full of the aggressive howls of dogs, and Taylor turned to his companion and said words to the effect that he was very surprised by the barking of the dogs, because he had walked along the same street the previous day without any barking from any dogs. His companion was black and informed Taylor that the dogs were barking because they had been trained to behave aggressively towards black people in the vicinity. Taylor was astonished. Professor Taylor's sociology had never attuned him to the fact that his whiteness conferred privileges, or indeed that he was publicly a white person and was thereby routinely treated differently from a black person, especially in a society as deeply racialized as South Africa.

This is the paradox of being white and 'seeing white', but being to all intents and purposes 'invisible' or, more appropriately, as Frankenberg, Garner, and other sociologists of 'whiteness' have suggested, 'unmarked'. In Western societies whites take being white for granted. Their particularity tends to be universalized. It is the default position from which the world is seen, but it also allows them to 'disappear' from the foreground of spaces and places, from their own streets to parks and shopping malls. Non-whites have a different experience in white-dominated societies. Their presence is noted as soon as they are sighted by white people (and by black people in certain occupations, such as the police force or security teams in areas like shopping malls).

In white-dominated societies, all spaces are racialized in favour of whites when compared to non-whites. This is one reason why whites often discount the experiences of non-whites when the latter complain about racism. Whites simply do not experience either what have come to be called the 'micro-aggressions' of everyday racism—habitually being followed by security guards in department stores is one extremely familiar experience; noticing the discomfort of white people in your presence is another—or the humiliation of being continually stopped and searched by police officers, having racist abuse shouted at you, and the knowledge that implicitly or explicitly you are being discriminated against at work, especially in the form of lower pay for the same work or being blocked when opportunities for promotion arise.

Often, the stock response to complaints about racial discrimination is disbelief and accusations of 'playing the race card', with the further accusation that race is being introduced by the non-white person where no racialization was present. The non-white person therefore stands accused of a perverse form of racism: 'reverse racism'.

In recent years there has been a growing interest and research in the emotional politics of white racism, and not only in the USA. In the UK, Reni Eddo-Lodge, in her book *Why I'm No Longer Talking to White People About Race*, discusses the discomfort, defensiveness, and even anger with which her white friends, acquaintances, and other white people react when she brings up issues concerning racism. She remarks, in particular, how white people simply fail to understand how they might be complicit, unwittingly, in shoring up structures of white dominance. In the American context, similar arguments are made in several books by black and white authors, for example *White Fragility*, *Silent Racism*, and *The Emotional Politics of Race*. In *Anger and Racial Politics*, Antoine J. Banks argues that Jim Crow-type disgust and repulsion in relation to blacks has been replaced by anger as the dominant emotion among whites in America. Theda Skocpol and Vanessa Williamson make a similar point when discussing the Tea Party supporters who formed the subject of their research, and especially the opposition of these supporters to President Obama's health care reforms.

Several overriding issues emerge from all this research. White people tend to have a sense that racism is a thing of the past, and when minorities of colour bring up issues of racism they are perceived as bringing in racialization where none existed before, hence the defensiveness and anger with which white people react during discussions of race and racism. There is a lack of understanding on white people's part that it is not just a question of their own individual prejudice or lack of it, but of how racism works in a systematic and structural form to disadvantage ethnic minorities. And there is a taken-for-granted lens and experience of whiteness which makes for ignorance and blindness to the discrimination that ethnic minorities suffer in white-dominated societies.

The white American author Tim Wise, in a variety of books, has addressed the issue of white privilege, a fact often unnoticed by white people, and has amassed a wide range of evidence from his own experience and from that of others. The reader is encouraged to read his books, mentioned in the guide to further reading, for elaboration. Similarly, the work of George Lipsitz, *The Possessive Investment in Whiteness* and other research, shows the advantages that accrue to American whites simply from the fact of their whiteness, leading to and reproducing generations of unfair advantage in housing, education, health, and employment.

The Gates affair

An instance which gained some global attention is worth mentioning. In July 2009 Professor Henry Louis Gates Jr, a famous scholar of African American studies at Harvard University, was arrested when trying to get access to his own house in a middle-class, predominantly white suburb. He had just arrived at his home after a trip to China and could not immediately locate the keys to his house. A white officer, Sergeant James Crowley, handcuffed and arrested him for breaking in, for by this stage Gates had already entered his home and was speaking on the phone. Having explained the situation to the police officer, the latter did not believe him, despite Professor Gates producing identification cards, including his driving licence, that showed Gates's photo and address, and a form of identification that showed his affiliation with Harvard University. The question obviously arises: would a white professor who provides identification about living in a property located in an affluent suburb have had to undergo the ordeal of Professor Gates? It seems highly unlikely. As Charles Ogletree demonstrated in his book, *The Presumption of Guilt*, the treatment of Professor Gates follows a long-established pattern in which African Americans are almost always presumed to be guilty rather than, as the law requires, presumed to be innocent. Ogletree documents the cases of other African American faculty and students at Harvard who have had similar experiences with the police, where the presumption is one of guilt rather than innocence. As we have seen, this is only the tip of an ugly iceberg, in which African

Americans and Hispanics experience stark discrimination in the American justice system.

Another notable example of how deviation from the norm of whiteness, and the collective negative racialization of 'people of colour' or non-whites, is the case of Jean Charles de Menezes, who was gunned down by British police in their search for the perpetrators of the July 2005 bombings in London. De Menezes was a Brazilian electrician of pale brown complexion and with dark, short, curly hair. The police were actually looking for Hussain Osman, a British man of Yemeni heritage. Here was a case of all non-whites being perceived as potential terrorists. There is little doubt that had de Menezes been blond and blue-eyed, he would not even have entered the police's surveillance radar. As Garner has commented, 'Th[is]…demonstrates that being or not being white can be a matter of life and death, and that those on the white side of the equation generally make the decisions that make it so.'

As mentioned earlier, the recent shooting of several black men and one boy in the USA by white officers has now given rise to outrage and campaigning movements against police racism, especially the Black Lives Matter movement. The acquittal of the neighbourhood watch coordinator George Zimmerman, after he shot the black teenager Trayvon Martin, followed by the death of two more African Americans, Michael Brown in Ferguson, and Eric Garner, who was filmed gasping 'I can't breathe' repeatedly while in a police neck-hold, in New York City, have been pivotal in the rise of Black Lives Matter.

The persistence of a gross black–white divide in the USA, and the continuing disadvantaged position of African Americans, has now led to the emergence of studies of 'whiteness', which are in turn inspiring research in the UK. This is because there is a growing recognition that unlike the sentiment in the majority population that their societies have an 'ethnic minority problem' (in earlier years, these societies were exercised by 'the Jewish Question'), it is they, whites, who also constitute a major problem, and that it is the culture of 'whiteness' embedded in institutions that requires deeper analysis. It is not surprising that this is not a view widely held by white people within white-majority societies.

Another reason for the growth of studies of whiteness is the recognition that it is likely that by 2050, if not earlier, 'whites' will comprise a minority in the USA (data from the American Census Bureau in 2015 put the year at 2044). In other words, there is likely to be a crisis of American whiteness. But who exactly is counted as 'white' in such predictions? 'White' is not by any means an unambiguous category in the USA. First, many of Latin American origin identify as white for census and other purposes. This population of Hispanic white-identifiers could grow, throwing doubt on the prognosis. Second, the Census Bureau's projections count people of 'mixed race' as an ethnic minority. But this may underestimate the proportion that will count as white in the future. Already, many Americans with one white parent identify as white or partly white, and Americans of Hispanic origin can choose more than one 'race'. Third, a quarter of Asians and Hispanics marry outside their 'race', and for American-born Asians this rate is nearly doubled. Thus, although the 'mixed-race' American population at present is some 7 per cent, it is bound to grow. The question arises regarding their children, who may marry whites, and their grandchildren, some of whom may marry whites too. At what point do people start counting as white even if their grandparents and great-grandparents were counted and identified as 'mixed race'? What would happen to the one-drop rule with regard to whites (the next section will discuss its deployment to identify the black population)?

It is worth highlighting several other issues that have emerged in the wake of the rise of studies of whiteness. Earlier studies, for example by Ruth Frankenberg in the USA and Ann Phoenix in the UK, demonstrated the extent to which many white people's taken-for-granted whiteness was only shaken after travel into multiracial urban areas. In other words, whiteness is relational, and regarded as the norm unless non-whites are encountered and their status as co-citizens acknowledged. Another notable feature is the white response, 'we don't have a race problem here', because of the low numbers of ethnic minorities in that area, implying that race is only an issue when non-whites arrive on the scene, which of course belies the manner in which race is equally an issue in the formation and reproduction of white neighbourhoods, for example by 'white flight', in white-dominated societies. A quotation from research in predominantly white semi-rural Leicestershire in the UK, where there had recently been an arrival of British South Asian families, sums up this sort of attitude. Asked about their South Asian neighbours, one resident remarked, 'They are as good as gold...we never see them'. However, other residents complained that the Asians kept to themselves, did not integrate into village activities, and were prone to having large gatherings in their big houses: this placed Asians in a double bind, damned by some if they kept to themselves and praised by others if they remained outside village life.

Sociological research in the USA has revealed that lighter-skinned African Americans and Mexican Americans earn more, complete more years in education, live in more integrated neighbourhoods, and have better mental health than darker-skinned African Americans and Mexican Americans, as Margaret Hunter, author of *Race, Gender and the Politics of Skin Tone*, points out. In understanding the widespread use of skin-lightening creams among black women in South Africa, the USA, the UK, and many other societies, from Brazil and the Philippines to Nigeria, Ghana, Kenya, and the Caribbean, the role of white colonialism by the British, Spanish, and Portuguese cannot be underestimated. In all their colonies, wealth, power, and beauty were the property of the white elite and the lighter-skinned children of intermarriages and illegal liaisons between white male colonizers and local women.

Skin-lightening products, especially those containing bleaching agents, can be highly toxic, and attempts have been made to ban such products in Nigeria, Kenya, Ghana, and South Africa. Some of the issues involved are also discussed in the essays brought together by Evelyn Glenn in *Shades of Difference*. For example, the World Health Organization estimated in 2011 that as many as 77 per cent of Nigerian women use lightening products 'on a regular basis'; but even Nigerian men use them to enhance their attractiveness. The oppressive preference for lighter skin shades in the Indian subcontinent, which as elsewhere affects women more than men, has more complex origins, including the caste system established in ancient times, and indeed has no conclusive explanation, but there is no doubt that the effects of white British colonialism had a very important role to play; again, it is important to note that Indian men are also using skin lighteners. Advertising and film and TV culture play a significant role, with female film stars, in soaps and in advertising for all products, much more likely to be fair skinned in India. And of course, there is heavy, direct advertising of skin-lightening products.

Elsewhere in Asia, in China and Japan, again there seems to have been a very longstanding preference for lighter-skinned women. Some of this can be attributed to a time when these societies were predominantly agrarian. Whiter shades of skin colour denoted that the women did not have to work outdoors, thus conflating skin colour with privilege, which then translated into 'beauty'. In much the same way, middle- and upper-class white women in Victorian times kept out of the sun or used umbrellas to shield themselves against its tanning effects.

Whiteness (and blackness) have been historically *created*, and it is necessary to understand some key insights into the formation of 'whiteness' and 'blackness', especially in the USA, although some of these are also applicable to the UK. In the USA, lighter-skinned 'black' women not only earn more, they are treated more leniently by the judicial system, as sociological research has demonstrated.

Political activism and the civil rights struggles of the 1960s and 1970s led to the adoption of the slogan 'Black is Beautiful' to counter the damaging effects on African Americans of hegemonic conceptions of white beauty, attractiveness, and indeed 'Americanness'. The stigma of dark skin left its mark on many black entertainers too, the singer Nina Simone being a notable example. Michael Jackson's transition from black to almost white via skin-lightening and cosmetic surgery was the cause of much controversy in America. These are only some of the best-known illustrations, but large sections of the black population in the USA and the Caribbean have to live and struggle with what is often called 'colourism'.

Black and white in the USA: the social formation of whiteness and blackness

The founding of the USA provides one of the clearest examples of the conflation between racial whiteness, nation, and citizenship. In 1790 an Act of Congress decreed that 'all free white persons' 'shall be entitled to the rights of citizenship'. While there was some discussion of whether Catholics and Jews should be given the same rights (they were), it seemed so 'natural' to exclude non-whites and women that the subject never came up. But crucially, the difficulties surrounding racial classification also meant that definitions of black and white remained indeterminate.

The term 'white' had begun as a designation for the European explorers, traders, and settlers who had expropriated the land of North America's indigenous peoples and, subsequently, had made Africans, as slaves, into their property. From the start, whiteness and property owning were conflated and then given legal expression. Legally, as property, black slaves counted, for purposes of the composition of the Electoral College by which the president was elected, as three-fifths of the population of a state, although of course they were not allowed to vote.

However, it was not long before the seemingly obvious categories of 'white' and 'black' began to throw up their own anomalies. The trigger for what has become a still-surviving anxiety about who is *really* white in the USA was the substantial immigration into the USA of *other* kinds of whites to the original settlers. Notions of different white races that were already common in Europe, as we have seen, soon proliferated in public discussions in 19th-century America.

Nearly one and a half million Irish, fleeing the famine of the 1840s, soon found themselves at the receiving end of racism from those already settled in the USA who regarded Anglo-Saxon whiteness as superior to that of the Celts.

Some of the descriptions attached to the Irish newcomers are revealing: 'low browed', 'savage', 'bestial', 'lazy', and 'wild' were just some of them. The similarity of this dehumanizing abuse to that directed at blacks and native American populations is obvious. Cartoonists habitually portrayed the Irish as ape-like, images that had been popular in England, accompanying the colonization of Ireland (see Figures 6 and 7).

But the Irish found themselves increasingly being used by employers against black and Chinese workers. Moreover, they began to promote their own whiteness, partly by attacking blacks. They opposed black suffrage and emancipation. They built up formidable political machines, and by the 1890s had come to dominate Democratic Party organizations in the large northern cities.

Over time, the Irish also helped to redefine the idea of the white race to include the Irish in a 'Celtic-Anglo-Saxon' race. They promoted a wider unity between people of English, Scotch-Irish, French, Welsh, German, and Irish ancestry as a new and improved American white race.

TWO FORCES.

6. Anti-Irish cartoon from the 1880s.

Subsequently, it was the Italian immigrants—and to some extent the Jews—who found themselves in an indeterminate position in the racial order between white and black. 'Dago' was a common racial slur for describing Italians, accompanied by suggestions of

THE IGNORANT VOTE—HONORS ARE EASY.

7. Equation of blacks and Irish in America. The Irish are depicted as more ape-like.

innate emotionality, overly demonstrative behaviour, and 'warped' habits of thought.

It was under the umbrella racial category of 'Caucasian' that the Irish, Italians, Poles, Germans, and all other populations of European origin found gradual acceptance as full members of the 'white' American race.

The history of whiteness in the USA in the period from the 1840s to the 1940s shows clearly that colour and racial categorization have a fluidity and instability very much at odds with the conceptions of strict and obvious biological difference implied by the notion of race. Moreover, the way in which the category of 'coloured' developed to describe all non-whites serves to highlight the manner in which whiteness became the racial norm in America and elsewhere. The domination by whites in the racial order came to be hidden.

However, blackness, no less than whiteness, has been and continues to be a socially constructed and therefore highly contentious racial description. In the USA, the one-drop rule came to predominate. The idea that any amount of African ancestry meant a classification as black appears to be unique to the USA, although in practice similar categorizations have been accepted in the UK and elsewhere. It is particularly noteworthy that the one drop (of black blood) legitimizes a biological view of race, still in practice being used to categorize black people, although many of them can and do 'pass' as 'white'.

It has been estimated that at least three-quarters of the black American population has some ancestry that is European or white. Approximately one-quarter also have American Indian ancestry. Estimates of whites with black ancestry vary widely, from 1 to 20 per cent. All figures are likely to be underestimates, given that much 'mixing' has gone officially undocumented.

With the end of the Civil War in 1865, in which the continuation of slavery had itself been an issue, the Thirteenth Amendment to the American constitution was passed, abolishing slavery. In states like Louisiana, South Carolina, Mississippi, and Arkansas anti-miscegenation laws banning black–white marriages came off the statute books.

But not for long. The continuing hatred of blacks and implacable hostility to their aspirations for equality led to widespread white fears about 'interracial' sexual liaisons spiralling out of control, as well as anxieties about economic competition from blacks who were now officially entitled to learn how to read. Thus several southern states adopted the so-called 'Black Codes' which prohibited blacks from entry into industrial and skilled work, confining them to field labour and sharecropping. This is an important issue. It demonstrates in stark fashion how racialized inequalities were embedded into the institutional fabric of American society, and is one reason why it is legitimate to use the concept of 'structural racism' or 'systemic racism', because inequalities in employment gave whites built-in advantages that were only exhanced by other forms of discrimination that were piled on top of each other.

For example, it is worth remembering that even in the northern states before the Civil War blacks were barred from hotels and places of entertainment, from skilled crafts and professional colleges, and segregated on trains and churches. They had to pay taxes, but they could not vote, serve on a jury, or even appear as witnesses in court.

Disastrously, in 1883 a US Supreme Court ruling allowed segregation with regard to all relations involving close personal contact. This allowed southern states to develop segregated schooling and separate facilities in trains, buses, libraries, parks, swimming pools, and other public amenities. 'Interracial' marriages could once again be legally prohibited.

Thus came into being the notorious 'Jim Crow' system of segregation, named after a 'blackface' character, played by whites, portraying blacks as lazy, idiotic, childlike, and happy. The revamped system of segregation was not only legally enforced, but also violently policed by the Ku Klux Klan and other vigilante groups. The lynching of 'uppity' blacks, especially those accused of insulting behaviour towards white women, became horrifyingly common. Between 1890 and 1900, it has been estimated by historians that there were over 1,100 lynchings.

In the light of the history sketched out above, it should be clear, counterintuitive though it may seem, that 'whiteness' (and 'blackness') is as much achieved as ascribed. It is equally clear that most white people in white-majority societies are unaware of this. Whiteness becomes a taken-for-granted fact and a limiting perspective from which issues of racism and ethnicity are approached. The labelling of non-white foods and clothes as 'ethnic', especially in western Europe, is a small but exceptionally telling example of this taken-for-granted whiteness. It implies that whiteness is not an ethnicity or a racialized category. But it most definitely is.

Colourblind racism

There is a growing agreement among scholars, for example Burke, Bonilla-Silva, and Wise, that the forms of racism that are now most prevalent, especially in the USA, are versions of 'colourblind racism'. This may seem like a contradiction in terms. If racism has usually involved reference to physical markers, especially skin colour, how can attitudes and practices that make no reference to skin colour be racist? It is helpful, then, to begin with Meghan Burke's definition of colourblind racism as it applies to the USA: 'Colourblind racism asserts that there are no real problems with racism in our society, that challenges stem from individuals rather than our institutions and collective thinking and behavior.' She continues: 'In this sense colourblindness is a defence of the status quo. It is also a defence of individuals who may sincerely believe that they operate without bias, or those who believe that no one has any more significant privileges or disadvantages than anyone else.'

The rise of colourblind racism is premised on the (mistaken) belief that almost all impediments to the housing, educational, and employment opportunities of African Americans and Hispanics have now been revoked in the wake of the civil rights legislation of the 1960s that removed many of the legal and semi-legal barriers that had denied African Americans and non-white Hispanics access to equal opportunities.

The colourblind myth was given empirical grounding by the research of the eminent African American sociologist William Julius Wilson. In *The Declining Significance of Race* (1980), *The Truly Disadvantaged* (1987), and subsequent publications, Wilson argued that the real dividing line in American society was no longer that between white and black, but between social classes. His research suggested that all working-class communities, white and black, had suffered more or less equally from the collapse of manufacturing in favour of the service sector, deindustrialization, and the outsourcing of jobs. If there was higher unemployment among African Americans, this was in large part due to a geographical mismatch which left them residing in inner-city areas rather than the outer suburbs where the new service-sector jobs were being primarily created.

The colourblind view was grounded in the perception that blacks, whites, and non-white Hispanics now operated on a level playing field, and that no special consideration was to be given to the 'racial' background of, say, applicants for jobs or college admission. On the basis of this perception, courts began to chip away at affirmative action policies that had legally obliged educational and other institutions to take into account the historic and continuing disadvantage under which African Americans and

Hispanics had had to face life. The implication was that the more poorly resourced schools attended by African Americans, their much poorer housing conditions, and their location in the lowest-income jobs was more and more a thing of the past.

Eduardo Bonilla-Silva labels this form of perspective an 'abstract liberalism' that strips the individual from the continuing socio-economic context of racialized disadvantage, together with allied beliefs that residential segregation, for example, was primarily the product of 'like attracting like' human nature, thus discounting the massive discrimination that African Americans had suffered in getting access to decent suburbs, even when they were able to afford them, because of the segregation policies practised by real estate brokers. African Americans had also been deliberately kept out of the huge suburbanization programme instituted by the Federal Housing Administration, which had resulted in all-white suburbs after World War II, a fact noted in a variety of histories and sociologies of whiteness, for example by George Lipsitz. The house building and the creation of interstate highways involved in the suburbs gave huge employment opportunities to white workers, while major manufacturers had also deliberately located plants to white areas. Attempts at residential integration, if made at all, had been vehemently opposed by white residents in most white suburbs. White suburban schools were better resourced because they were funded on the basis of property values, which of course were much higher in the all-white suburbs. Moreover, the post-war GI bill which had given ex-service personnel who had fought in the war easier access to college and other forms of education discriminated heavily in favour of whites.

In the 1970s there was a greater ethnic diversification of suburbs, but this led to waves of 'white flight', which led to the collapse of property values and thus schooling resources now that African Americans, Hispanics, and Asians were moving in, while employment opportunities declined as the process of deindustrialization took its toll.

In other words, the idea that there was, in 1980s America, more and more of a level playing field in housing, educational resources, and employment opportunities was a myth. Research has documented that even well-off African Americans were living in urban areas that were considerably worse in all respects when compared to the neighbourhoods lived in by working-class whites. Students of colour are considerably more likely to be put on lower tracks in schools or labelled as learning disabled on flimsy evidence, as research cited by Wise and others has documented. Unemployment rates even among African American college graduates were considerably and stubbornly higher than for white graduates, and there continued to be a severe wealth gap between white and black families.

So, for people of colour to even make it to the point where they could be considered for college admission, or employment in managerial or professional occupations, they had to overcome obstacles that white admissions tutors and employers simply did not have to face and remained unaware of. Residential segregation has meant that whites and people of colour have perforce lived 'parallel lives', thereby creating ignorance of the real-life experiences of people of colour.

Treating all peoples as having equal opportunities means that failure can be attributed to individual deficiencies, and when failure is endemic in whole communities, the tendency is to blame the community. Thus an explanation has arisen—the 'culture of poverty' thesis—which has painted the African American community, especially, as suffering from a cultural deficit of single-parent families, low educational aspirations, laziness, and 'welfare dependency', and which, together or singly, explains the continuing disadvantaged position of African Americans in particular. President Reagan, especially, was involved in creating the stereotype of the 'Welfare Queen' living it up on benefits and breeding without thought. The myths have all been rebutted by rigorous empirical research. There are more single-parent black families, for example, simply because married African Americans have been having less children, thus proportionately expanding the numbers of African Americans born out of wedlock. Black pupils are more likely than their white counterparts to discuss school grades with parents, thus quashing the myth of lack of interest in education. Direct discrimination against African Americans by employers continues to be repeatedly documented by studies in which identical CVs are sent but with one bearing an obviously African American name and the other a white name. The latter is at least twice as likely to be called for interview, despite equivalent qualifications and employment experience. One study even found that a white with a criminal record was more likely to be called for interview than an equally qualified African American without a criminal record.

Colourblind racism has also been labelled 'laissez faire racism' because it is based on the myth of individuals with equal starting points competing in a free market, thus chiming with neoliberal economic nostrums. Indeed, it has been argued by Randolph Hohle that processes of racialization have been crucially intertwined with the rise of neoliberal economic policies that involve the deregulation of markets and the shrinking of the state sector, especially in the area of welfare. In effect, neoliberal policies have served to reproduce white privilege.

The culture of poverty thesis is often underpinned by the myth of the 'model minority' as applied to the supposed success of Asian Americans. This is how the argument goes: if people of colour are discriminated against, how is it that Asian Americans have been so successful? But this line of reasoning ignores the fact that only a small proportion of Asian Americans embody the American dream of individual effort and community strength leading to economic success. As research cited by Burke, Wise, Bonilla-Silva, and others shows, the 'Asian American success story' ignores the large swathes of the Asian American population that have not succeeded: those of Vietnamese, Cambodian, Thai, Korean, and even Chinese origin.

The election of Barack Obama

If racism is so deeply embedded, institutionally and culturally, in the American nation, how was it possible for Barack Hussein Obama, a 'biracial' man who identified as black and had married a black woman, to win election to the highest office in the land? Not just once, but twice? In each election, one of the issues that worked in Obama's favour was that even some poor whites were able to identify with an Ivy League-educated black man and his equally well-qualified wife because both had grown up in poor and straitened circumstances. Barack Obama had known how it felt to have food put on the table with the assistance of (welfare) food stamps. Michelle Obama had grown up in the deprived South Side of Chicago in a one-bedroom apartment. Both had succeeded with determined hard work. Neither could be accused of laziness or being welfare dependent, the deeply held stereotypes that plague the lives of African Americans. There were special circumstances too. In 2008 Obama's early opposition to the unpopular Iraq war, and his pledge to close the discredited detention centre at Guantanamo Bay, played well to the voting public.

However, it was Obama's 'softly softly' approach to race that was decisive. Whether in his earlier best-selling books or in his campaigns, Obama made it clear that he was not in favour of race-specific policies. To put it bluntly, he ducked the question of racism in American society. He consistently favoured 'universalist' policies, based on the notion espoused by earlier successful presidential nominees, that 'a rising tide lifts all boats'. That is, raise the incomes and general circumstances of all in poor circumstances, and blacks will also benefit, but not at the perceived expense of whites. What this did was not scare white voters who might have otherwise thought that Obama was out to get revenge for all the injustices suffered by African Americans over the centuries. He took away the fear of the angry black man.

At the end of 'eight years in power', to borrow the title of the award-winning black journalist Ta-Nehisi Coates's highly critical book on Obama's presidency, African Americans' hopes that a black president would finally fight their corner from the most powerful position in the system were dashed. Cornel West, another influential African American intellectual, denounced Obama as just another neoliberal who had failed black America.

Wise, in his 2010 book, accused Obama of being a major promoter of the myth of a colourblind 'post-racial' America, a phrase that had been much bandied about by white commentators, who proclaimed that the election of Obama showed that America had moved beyond 'race' into a definitively post-racial era in which now even a black American could be president.

The critiques of Obama by Coates, West, and Wise have the weight of evidence supporting them. But it is worth remembering what happened on the occasions when Obama did raise the issue of race from a black perspective. One was when he called the act of the arrest of Professor Gates 'stupid'. Another was when, after Trayvon Martin was shot dead carrying only a can of soda and a snack, President Obama ruminated publicly that had he had a son, he would have looked like Martin, adding later that thirty-five years ago he would have looked like Trayvon Martin.

Both sets of remarks, on Gates and Martin, unleashed a vile, vicious, primarily right-wing racist backlash against Obama that gave an indication of what might have happened if Obama had fought his campaigns and based his policies with the explicit intention of righting the racist wrongs of the past. Mild though Obama's observations were, all the tropes of the angry black man out to get revenge were thrown at him, especially in talk shows on radio and TV, with Rush Limbaugh and Glenn Beck leading the charge. Among other things, Obama's policies were accused of being covert attempts at getting 'reparations' for slavery, segregation, and discrimination. If earlier Coates had praised Obama's 'genius' and 'remarkable ability to soothe race consciousness among whites', he now came to realize what might have been the consequences of a more 'race conscious' president.

The idea that policies based on a 'rising tide lifts all boats' attitude would help African Americans just as much as aiding the upward mobility of whites also needs to be scrutinized. As Coates has pointed out, the evidence suggests that all ladders are not equal, 'that to be a member of the "black race" had specific, quantifiable consequences. Not only did poor blacks tend to be much less likely to advance up their ladder, but those who did stood a much greater likelihood of tumbling back.' Also, while whites often brought with them wealth accumulated over the generations, such as 'the home of a deceased parent, a modest inheritance, a gift from a favourite uncle', blacks in the middle class 'often brought with them generational debt—an incarcerated father, an evicted niece, a mother forced to take in her sister's kids'.

However, whites too are divided by class and gender: hence the need to explore the idea of intersectionality.

Chapter 6
Intersectionality and 'implicit' or 'unconscious' bias

Race, class, and gender were often referred to as the 'holy trinity' of sociological analysis in the 1980s, because it was becoming clear that racial inequalities needed to be considered in relation to both class and gender. White working-class men and women, after all, although they may have been earning more than their ethnic minority counterparts, were nevertheless disadvantaged in relation to white middle- and upper-class men and women. Middle-class black men would be eyed with suspicion and often stopped and searched in white suburbs that were largely the domain of middle-class white women and men.

Intersectionality studies

This 'mantra' of race, class, and gender has now led to a new and to some extent almost separate field of research under the umbrella term of 'intersectionality' studies, which includes within its research framework an understanding that age, disability, and citizenship also have differential impacts on majority and minority communities and individuals.

Intersectionality studies gained their first impetus in the USA, as black women began to challenge white feminists with disregarding the further disadvantage in economic inequality, power, and dignity in social interactions that black women suffered. This point had been made by earlier black women activists, for example Sojourner Truth (who had been a slave and had escaped with her daughter but had had to leave three children behind), whose pained cry of 'Ain't I a woman?' had been uttered in the middle of the 19th century. The insight became incorporated into black women's activism from the 1970s onwards in response to white women's 'second wave' feminism.

Two prominent African American female academics and activists whose work has been particularly influential in intersectionality studies are Kimberley Crenshaw and Patricia Hill Collins. In a recent co-authored book, Collins defines the guiding principle underlying intersectionality studies in the following manner: 'When it comes to social inequality, people's lives and the organization of power in a given society are better understood as being shaped not by a single axis of social division, be it race or gender or class, but by many axes that work together *and influence each other*. Intersectionality as an analytic tool gives people better access to the complexity of the world and themselves' (my emphasis).

I have singled out the phrase 'and influence each other' to highlight the fact that intersectionality cannot be understood in an 'additive' way, combining race, class, and gender as if they were separate 'variables' amenable to statistical analysis in any particular case to find out which of these three contributes what amount to an individual's income, social status, probability of incarceration, and so forth. Such a method would assume that race, class, and gender develop separately from each other and then come together to impact on an individual. However, class is racialized, as is gender, and race is classed and gendered. All three become formative influences in any individual's life from the start, and then have variable influences at different life stages and in different social, cultural, interactional, and institutional contexts. I will refer to this process as *intersectional-interformation*. Sociologists and activists—there has been a continuous interaction between them, for some academic sociologists are also activists, and some activists have studied sociology—have realized, as I discussed earlier, that age, disability, and citizenship are also significant dimensions, and so these are now also included as intersectional-interformation features in people's lives.

Given that most intersectional studies have focused on the situation of women of various backgrounds, contrastingly I will focus mainly on how intersectionality throws light on the situation of African American men, and the formation of working-class African American masculinity. This is to underscore that although most research has been on women, men's situations and life histories are also only properly understandable through an intersectional lens.

Take the case of Eric Garner, a 43-year-old African American male who was arrested for illegally selling loose cigarettes on the street in Staten Island in 2014. He died on the pavement because of a chokehold by a police officer. The incident was filmed, and Garner was heard to say eleven times, 'I can't breathe', but the police officer did not loosen his chokehold for some time. A decision was made not to charge the police officer in a court hearing before a grand jury. The proceedings and the charge against the police officer were kept secret, but it would not be too fanciful to imagine that the police officer's defence would have included the view that he feared Garner, that he posed a danger, and that the police officer was acting in self-defence.

Garner was a working-class African American male who, by all accounts, was not dangerous. Indeed, Garner was a family man who had been a horticulturalist with the New York City Department of Parks and Recreation and had had to retire because of poor health. Friends described him as generous, friendly, and 'a neighbourhood peacemaker', although he had been arrested several times, mainly for selling unlicensed cigarettes. Just before his arrest, he had broken up a fight, which is perhaps how he had come to police notice at that fateful time. How had he come to be seen as dangerous? To understand that, we have to analyse the common experiences of African American young males, younger, that is, than Garner was at the time he was killed, to put together a narrative of how lower-class (but also to some extent middle-class) black identities and their perceptions among white law enforcers come to be constructed.

Here, the death of another African American male provides some important clues: Trayvon Martin was a 17-year-old who was visiting his father's fiancée, with his dad, in a gated community in Sanford, Florida. Martin lived with his mother in Florida. Martin was shot to death by George Zimmerman, a mixed-race Hispanic man who was a neighbourhood watch coordinator for the same gated community, which had suffered burglaries in the period preceding the death. Martin was walking back from a local store where he had bought some snacks. Zimmerman was not on duty, but driving on an errand, and on spotting Martin, called the Sanford police, stating that 'a real suspicious guy' was walking around ostensibly not to any purpose, but looked like he was on drugs and looking into homes. Significantly, Zimmerman reported that the 'suspicious guy' was wearing a hoodie (it was raining), and said, as recorded by police, that 'these assholes, they always get away'.

Zimmerman reported that the young man was running, but he was given strict instructions not to follow Martin and that police officers were on their way. Zimmerman agreed to stop looking for Martin. But for reasons that are not entirely clear, an altercation took place between the two in which Zimmerman shot Martin dead not far from where Martin was staying. Zimmerman told the officers who arrived that he had been acting in self-defence and he did appear to have some bleeding and superficial injuries. Zimmerman was held for questioning, but after five hours was released because, the police chief said, there was no evidence to refute Zimmerman's account of events leading up to the shooting.

The events and legal and eye-witness accounts leading up to Zimmerman's trial are too complicated to explore here. But there was considerable anger in black communities, and even President Obama intervened in the debates, saying that if he had a son, 'he would look like Trayvon'. After a trial, Zimmerman was found not guilty of second-degree murder. Subsequently, President Obama gave a press conference in which he complained about black men being unfairly racially profiled, and said that Trayvon Martin 'could have been me 35 years ago', as quoted earlier.

Geraldo Rivera, a host on the Fox News Channel, claimed that 'gangsta style clothing' was as much responsible for the death as Zimmerman, and followed up with 'I am urging the parents of black and Latino youngsters, particularly, to not let their children go out wearing hoodies'.

The *Washington Post* and *ABC News* conducted a nationwide poll which revealed, much as public opinion polls had revealed during the trial of the black athlete O. J. Simpson, that nearly 90 per cent of African Americans thought the shooting was unjustified, but only 33 per cent of whites came to the same conclusion.

What has this got to do with intersectionality?

Eric Garner was black, male, and working class: three characteristics that combine and intersect in stereotypes of aggressive and dangerous African American men.

As Romero and many others have pointed out, police racial profiling of young black and Hispanic males highlights 'urban' dress. This includes baggy jeans, T-shirt, baseball caps worn backwards, and *hooded sweatshirts*. This is why, in my account of the events leading up to the shooting of Trayvon Martin, I emphasized both that he was wearing a 'hoodie' and that *Fox News* hosts and others focused attention on hoodies as symbolic of black and Hispanic young male alienation, aggression, and criminality. Romero cites research which shows how encounters with police *shape*, in what I have called an intersectional-interformational process, particular forms of black and Hispanic masculinity. What she calls 'hyper-masculinity' *emerges* in the context of racialized, gendered, and classed encounters that black and Hispanic young men have with police, probation officers, and others in authority in detention facilities. In turn, these encounters have led to expectations among detained youth of displaying the characteristics of 'real men', which earns them respect, and this type of masculinity also becomes a general survival strategy for gaining respect in dangerous neighbourhoods and in prison.

Add to this data from the US Department of Education which show that black boys are treated as suspects three times more often than white boys (and black girls are suspected six times more than white girls). Moreover, given that the evidence shows that black boys are expelled at ten times the rate of white boys, which is more likely to lead to them hanging around on the streets where they are then more likely to have encounters with police, with a high chance of these interactions leading eventually to arrest, prison, criminal records that hinder employment chances, and so forth, and we get some idea of the *systematic* processes by which black men end up being disadvantaged from generation to generation while also developing forms of hyper-masculine identity which leads to justifications for treating them as dangerous. While Eric Garner and Trayvon Martin were not necessarily caught up in such a process, the manner in which they were viewed as potentially threatening—as a large black male engaging in minor illegal activity (that albeit did not involve violence of any sort), or 'wearing a hoodie while black'—can only be understood by way of an intersectional-interformational analysis.

While I do not have the space to analyse in detail how black and Hispanic women's intergenerational inequalities and stereotypes can also only be understood in an intersectional analytical framework, I will point up how a top black woman sportswoman, the tennis star Serena Williams, has been treated, to give an understanding of how her gender has been racialized. Although Williams twice beat Maria Sharapova in Grand Slam tournaments in 2015, Williams earned $12 million in endorsements while Sharapova earned $29 million. Williams has had to suffer a continuous barrage of insults against her femininity because of her muscular build. The argument is constantly made that she *only* succeeds because of her 'unfeminine' body, not her astonishing tennis talent and hard work, and her wins are followed by a Twitter-storm of racial hate speech. I have already referred to Roseanne Barr's 'planet of the apes' comment, and it bears repeating that Michelle Obama was regularly compared to a gorilla. The intersection of gender with a particularly old trope of racialization does not spare black women, no matter what their status and accomplishments.

Intersectionality is an indispensable framework for understanding how dimensions of unequal racial, gendered, and classed economic, cultural, and power relations are institutionalized and reproduced.

In the case of Hispanic women, findings from the Institute for Women's Policy Research revealed that in 2009, while white women earned on average 75 per cent of what white men earned, Hispanic women earned only 52.9 per cent.

'Implicit' and 'unconscious' bias

Coming back to black men, one explanation for the shooting of unarmed black men by American police officers of the kind considered earlier in this chapter is that their acts were committed because of an 'implicit' bias or 'unconscious' bias against black people. The term 'racism' is rarely used in this context, a practice which is itself of some interest.

On 12 April 2018 two black men sat down at a branch of Starbucks in Philadelphia and waited for a white business associate to join them. A few minutes earlier they had been refused a request by one of them to use the bathroom. They did not order any food or drink when asked whether they wanted to, saying they would order when their business associate arrived and joined them. The manager of the branch immediately rang the police, who arrived at the same time as the white business associate who corroborated the story that he was there to meet with the two black men.

The police arrested the two black men, handcuffed them, and marched them off to a detention facility. The arrests were recorded on a white customer's cell phone and the video went viral, unleashing outrage among large swathes of the American nation who saw this as a blatant and typical case of American racism faced by African Americans. The two 23-year-olds had been harassed by police officers before, although they had not been arrested. They spent several hours in jail, not knowing their fate, and were obviously not aware that their arrest was being widely viewed with anger online. That weekend protests at the branch of Starbucks took place, and a national boycott of Starbucks was called for.

Starbucks management apologized and ordered all branches to close for mandatory diversity training to tackle 'unconscious' bias; a similar programme was subsequently implemented in Canadian Starbucks stores. What Starbucks—and many other corporations and institutions—called 'unconscious' bias has also been labelled 'implicit' bias, especially in the discipline of social psychology which has more or less taken ownership of the concept. 'Unconscious' racism is also used, although as we shall see social psychologists are reluctant to use 'racism' or 'racist' as descriptors. 'Diversity training' is often the term used to describe the 'debiasing' programmes, and a multi-million-dollar industry has grown up to offer diversity training in the USA, but also in the UK and elsewhere. Diversity training is mandatory in many private and state institutions.

In the UK, the Parole Board, the body responsible for deciding whether prisoners can be released into the community, announced in November 2018 that it had no black members. The chair of the board, Caroline Corby, is reported to have said that she fears that 'unconscious' bias may account for the absence of black members and the low numbers of ethnic minority individuals recruited by the Parole Board. In November 2018, Richard Hastings, a black IT manager in the British NHS, working at the King's College Hospital NHS trust, was awarded £1 million in damages for racial discrimination after an internal inquiry tribunal found that he had been the victim of 'unconscious' bias (as reported in the *Guardian* newspaper on 23 November 2018).

In December 2018 the *Guardian* ran a series of articles, based on commissioned polling, to reveal the persistence and effects of what it explicitly called 'unconscious' racial bias. The newspaper directly confronted the problems surrounding the *concept* of 'unconscious' and 'implicit' bias in an article on 2 December by its science correspondent, Hannah Devlin, but did not deem some of the criticisms of this framework as being of sufficient merit to prevent a team of *Guardian* journalists from undertaking a project that took 'unconscious' bias as its guiding concept, together with all its attendant theoretical underpinnings.

The findings were headlined, 'Revealed: the stark evidence of everyday racial bias in Britain', and make for salutary reading. The poll compared the experiences of 1,000 people from ethnic minority backgrounds with a similar number of white people. According to the *Guardian*, 'the poll found comprehensive evidence to support concerns that unconscious bias has a negative effect on the lives of Britain's 8.5 million' BAME people. Among the findings were that 38 per cent of ethnic minority people said that they had been wrongly suspected of shoplifting in the last five years compared with 14 per cent of white people, with black people and women more likely to be targeted; one in seven of those from ethnic minorities said they had been treated as a potential shoplifter compared to one in twenty-five white people in the last month; minorities were more than twice as likely to have encountered abuse or rudeness from a stranger in the last week and one in eight had heard racist language directed at them in the month before they were surveyed; 53 per cent of people from a minority background believed they had been treated differently because of their hair, clothes, or appearance, compared with 29 per cent of white people; 41 per cent of ethnic minority people said someone had assumed they were not British at some point in the last year because of their ethnicity. Moreover, 57 per cent of minorities said that they felt they had to work harder than white people to succeed, and 40 per cent said that they earned less or had worse employment prospects because of their ethnic background.

Many of these subjective perceptions were complemented by more objective measures of racially biased outcomes. BAME unemployment, at 6.3 per cent, was considerably higher than white unemployment, which stood at 3.6 per cent (these statistics are different from the ones available in October 2018 which I cited earlier). The figures are not broken down by gender and ethnicity, including religious background within BAME communities, thus preventing any form of intersectional analysis.

Other objective measures revealed that the London Metropolitan Police use stun guns and tasers four times more against black than white people, which were said to stem from assumptions by the police that black people are more dangerous. In my discussion of intersectionality, I discussed how such perceptions can result in a self-fulfilling cycle which means that disproportionately more black people than white end up in prison or lose their lives while being arrested or being in police custody.

Black women and men from ethnic minorities, the *Guardian* survey also reported, are less likely than white men to pass driving tests, an outcome that was squarely blamed on racial bias as there is no evidence that ethnic background affects an individual's driving skills. Here, although the *Guardian* does not take this obvious step, intersectional analysis is clearly significant, because the data also reveal that female pass rates have been consistently lower than those of men, although the data also reveal that women drivers were less likely to be involved in road accidents. The majority of driving testers are white and male.

Many of these cases and events may sound like the outcome of the 'unwitting racism' that was identified by the Macpherson Report's damning account of institutional racism. However, this is not necessarily the case because, as I will argue shortly, the presuppositions underlying the concept of 'implicit' and 'unconscious' 'bias' are ahistorical and individualist rather than embedded in a proper institutional and structural context.

First, though, what is 'implicit' bias or 'unconscious' bias? The term 'implicit racism' is more rarely used; 'bias' is a more comfortable and innocuous idea than racism. The conceptual underpinnings of 'unconscious' bias, which, for convenience, is the term I shall use, in line with the usage in social psychology and 'diversity training' (I shall now drop the quotation marks), is very akin to the ideas popularized in *Thinking, Fast and Slow* by the Nobel laureate Daniel Kahneman. He argued that in making decisions, our cognitive structure is such that in the first instance a decision is made effortlessly, relying on intuition and information that is more easily available to the brain; only later does the brain make the more effortful attempt to think the decision through more thoroughly and slowly, using more information that requires more concentration and consideration.

Social psychologists who have developed the idea of implicit bias argue in similar fashion that when, say, a white individual first encounters (in everyday life, on an appointments committee, or as a police officer) a black or other ethnic minority person, her or his brain immediately goes into intuitive mode and draws upon stereotypes that are easily available in the brain's storage cupboard, so to speak. This may or may not be followed by a more considered judgement which challenges the stereotype. If the latter mode of judgement does not follow, the white individual is most likely to act on the basis of the stereotype. If the stereotypes that are immediately available are negative, and in fact the evidence shows that in white-dominated societies there are more negative than positive stereotypes of black people especially, then the white individual is more likely to react negatively and treat the black individual in an inferior manner, whether this is in terms of a job offer, following a black shopper in a store, encountering a young black man on the police beat, deciding whether or not to stop a driver for a minor traffic offence, and so forth. A key reference point in the study of 'unconscious' bias is the book *Blindspot* by Mahzarin R. Banaji and Anthony G. Greenwald, social psychologists at Harvard.

The statistics for police stop and search in the USA and the UK, as shown earlier, show an extraordinarily disparate treatment by officers of young—and often of obviously middle-class, well-dressed, briefcase-carrying—black males. The case of Professor Henry Louis Gates of Harvard University, cited earlier, is a textbook example of how unconscious bias operates in practice even against professional, well-spoken, middle-aged, upper-middle-class black men in the USA.

Social psychologists have devised a series of 'implicit association tests' (IATs) that can be taken online, whereby individuals are asked to make quick-fire responses to images which initially are not of black and white individuals, but soon progress to images which supposedly trigger negative responses to black people and positive ones to whites. In many institutions, both private and public, IATs have become mandatory, as have diversity awareness programmes which supposedly counteract 'implicit' or 'unconscious' racial bias. The case of Starbucks management closing their stores and asking all employees to undergo diversity training is a good example of how the ideas of 'unconscious' bias, and the supposed remedy, diversity training, are becoming an ingrained and almost automatic response to cases of obvious discrimination against black and ethnic minority people.

The theoretical underpinnings of the concept of implicit bias are shaky. But before exposing those to critical analysis, let us look at the evidence for the effectiveness of diversity training based on the idea of unconscious bias. The research evidence, ably summarized in Jonathan Kahn's *Race on the Brain: What Implicit Bias Gets Wrong About the Struggle for Racial Justice* and in many publications by other critics, is that diversity training is highly *ineffective* as a tool for combating racial prejudice.

There are several problems that researchers have highlighted about the flaws that have now been revealed in diversity training. Training programmes vary widely, from just watching a video, to six-hour modules involving role play. Employees often resent mandatory training and are therefore resistant to learning any of the lessons regarding implicit bias. The content of videos and longer modules is often forgotten within days and even hours after attendance at a diversity-training exercise. Often, racist views are not necessarily challenged but further reinforced during the programme. Moreover, highlighting the widespread existence of bias often simply leads to individual participants expressing their bias and feeling justified by the evidence of bias in a self-reinforcing cycle. In many cases, participants and institutions regard this a box-ticking exercise, with no attempt being made to get feedback or implement follow-up programmes. Researchers often cite, for illustration, the 2015 case of a Texas police officer, Eric Casebolt, who had undergone extensive diversity training, as well as attending seminars on racial profiling, but soon after was filmed violently assaulting a black female teenager in an altercation at a pool party; he never faced any charges. This is only one among many case studies available in the critical research literature.

The coyness that surrounds any mention of *racism* in IATs, diversity-training programmes, and in the research of those social psychologists who champion IATs and diversity training is symptomatic of flaws in their wider conceptual assumptions, and the lack of historical, institutional, and social understanding of how racism operates, all of which have been exposed by critics.

A major problem in 'unconscious' bias research is that racial bias is understood as on a par with any other bias, for example supporting a local sports team. But this is to completely marginalize and trivialize the horrific history of racism that is revealed by studies of slavery, the Holocaust, Jim Crow segregation, and so forth, and the explicit racist assumptions that are routinely articulated by ordinary white citizens in white-dominated societies. Instead of focusing on structural and systemic racism embedded over generations in cultures and institutional practices, IATs and diversity training see bias as simply individual prejudice and an individual failing, an irrational pathology that can be cured by diversity training. This has been a wider problem in psychological and social psychological studies of 'prejudice', well explored in the book *Beyond Prejudice* mentioned in Chapter 4.

There is, too, a fetishization of measurement techniques for the results of IATs, with an insufficient understanding of what the results actually mean and reveal. Thus, the champions of IATs and diversity training within social psychology, and the burgeoning diversity-training industry, explicitly believe that their measurement techniques will reveal how racism is diminishing, and will thus provide scientific proof of when affirmative action programmes will no longer be necessary.

As Kahn has pointed out, such assumptions are based on the view that the goal of any form of anti-racist education is colourblindness. The goal of anti-racism is said to be reached when individuals treat other individuals in neutral terms. But what this highlights is that the proponents of IATs want white individuals to treat black people as if they were white, on the assumption that such a change would create a level playing field. But this is to miss the point that black people and members of ethnic minorities will have come to any encounter with, say, a white manager or police officer, having experienced myriad forms of racialized discrimination. A manager in a corporation, just as much as an admissions tutor at a university, has to grasp, in fact, that the person who appears before them has had to overcome, on average, worse childhood living conditions, poorer schooling with fewer resources, countless rejections after interviews, or not having had any interviews at all because of racialized discrimination. *Whiteness* in fact is the norm that is further reinforced and is deeply embedded in the underlying theoretical underpinnings of implicit bias research.

No wonder that Kahn, who had already published his *Race on the Brain* when the Starbucks events took place, argued on 23 April 2018 in an article in the Minneapolis newspaper *Star Tribune* that the Starbucks incidents demonstrated not unconscious or implicit bias but were clear cases of racism. He asks, first, 'why did the Starbucks employee feel compelled to call police to remove two men who were "trespassing" when they were not being disruptive and explained they were waiting for a friend?' Second, 'why did the police respond with massive force (I counted seven officers in the video), handcuff the two men and then arrest them?'

His firm and damning conclusion is as follows:

> The other patrons in the video did not need 'implicit bias training' to see the[se] actions for what they were: racism . . . The incident does not simply reflect the misguided 'unconscious stereotypes' held

by a few benighted individuals. Rather, it exemplifies the broader systemic and structural problem of using police to enforce racial boundaries and hierarchies in public places . . . Diversity training is a multi-billion-dollar-a-year industry that has been around for decades. It makes people feel good, assuring them, like self-help gurus do, that they are working to become the best nonbiased version of themselves they can be.

He adds later: 'Diversity management . . . does more to insulate businesses from lawsuits than to increase the representation of minorities in the workforce or reduce the frequencies of incidents such as what occurred at Starbucks.'

The chair of the UK Parole Board should take note, as should all those who believe racism is the product of implicit or unconscious bias and that the remedy for it is diversity training. The *Guardian*'s analysis, although dependent upon the concept of 'unconscious' bias, does not discus diversity training except in passing.

However, the conclusion should not be drawn that evidence from studies based on unconscious bias, like those of Britain's *Guardian* newspaper, should simply be set aside as of no significance. Rather, they can complement the results from analyses of structural and systematic racism. The *Guardian*'s account of racial bias, for instance, is particularly useful in highlighting what are called the 'micro-aggressions' of what is also referred to as 'everyday racism', such as racial abuse on the street or while using public transport, the throwing of banana skins at football players, and the myriad other discriminatory experiences of ethnic minorities, such as being disproportionately suspected of shoplifting (but which also affects more women than men from all backgrounds), and the evident discomfort felt by some white people when forced to sit next to a black person or a hijab-wearing woman.

A selection of quotations from ethnic minorities, published in the *Guardian* on 8 December 2010, give a flavour of the kind of racism that is routinely and continuously part of the experiences of ethnic minorities in Britain. The quotations that follow are themselves selected from the many sent in by BAME readers:

I was working for a very well-known clothing retailer and standing next to the manager as she looked through CVs . . . [she threw out] all the ones with names she didn't recognize . . . the shortlist had nobody with a non-English first name, despite well over 50% of the original pile being made up of people with Asian or African names. It made me feel very uncomfortable. I took no further action as I felt I was not in a position to challenge this behavior.

When I tell white people I'm an English teacher, they always make it clear I couldn't possibly be teaching their children English by saying 'Is that English as a second language?' The sub-text is: 'How is it possible for someone who looks like you to teach English?' My white colleagues do not get asked similar questions.

I hate shopping in department stores as I've experienced being followed by a security guard. I earn enough to buy items I touch, but if I have to go shopping I usually don't carry a large handbag now, to ensure I'm not followed.

The following is an extract from an article of 2 December 2018 by Afua Hirsch, the *Guardian*'s British-born mixed-heritage journalist; Hirsch's book *Brit(ish)* contains many more examples:

Has [racism] evolved into something hidden by the politeness of well-meaning British behaviour? What I call 'the question', for example: 'Where are you from?' And to keep on asking, until information about some supposedly exotic country of origin is delivered. The kindly claim by a friend that you are fine, because 'we don't really see you as black', or the patient explanation delivered by a colleague: 'I am not being racist, you just can't get a job round here any more if you are white' . . . In my book, I recall going into a high-end shop on my local high street . . . only to be told I wasn't welcome because 'black girls steal'.

Her book describes, among other things, how she has been mistaken for Michelle Obama despite looking nothing like her. Or, less flatteringly, at Oxford University, college porters constantly asking for identification to confirm that she genuinely was a student at Oxford University, an indignity described by a very large number of black students at Oxford and Cambridge.

Everyday racism is the subject of excellent accounts in Andrew Smith's *Racism and Everyday Life*, Philomena Essed's *Understanding Everyday Racism*, and the edited collection *The Good Immigrant*.

In December 2018 Britain's Equality and Human Rights Commission launched an inquiry into the large amount of racial harassment faced by black and ethnic minority students at British universities. To take just one of the many reported incidents, Nottingham Trent University student Joe Tivnan had to pay £500 compensation to fellow student Rufaro Chisango after racist chanting that was captured on video and went viral. Among his chants was 'We hate blacks'.

While on the subject of British higher education, it is worth highlighting that in November 2018 it had already been revealed by the Universities and College Employers Association that black male academic staff are paid around 13 per cent less on average than white academics of a similar age and education. In Chapter 1 I cited the *Guardian* newspaper's evidence from a freedom of information enquiry that suggests a great degree of racism at UK universities.

Juxtaposing the experience of everyday, routine racism with the stark facts of ethnic minority disadvantage in a great many spheres of life shows how everyday racism and structural, systemic racism combine to 'lock in' ethnic minority disadvantage.

The treatment of American media magnate and broadcaster Oprah Winfrey in Switzerland demonstrates that wealth and fame provide no protection to black people against everyday racism when their true wealth and status are unknown. They experience the same racism as other black people.

The Swiss tourism board was forced to apologize to her after she revealed that a shop assistant had refused to show her a handbag that Winfrey was interested in on the grounds that 'it is too expensive'. As Winfrey insisted on seeing the bag, the shop assistant said, according to Winfrey's own account of the incident, 'No, no, no. You don't want to see that one . . . because that one will cost too much, you will not be able to afford that one.' Oprah Winfrey is a multi-billionaire; the bag cost $38,000.

Chapter 7

The rise of right-wing national populism and the future of racism

I wrote the first edition of this book in 2006, before the great recession of 2008 and its aftermath of 'austerity' which has hit poor communities particularly hard, and before the onward march of globalization and deindustrialization that has hollowed out even more towns and cities in Europe and the USA. To these drivers of nationalist reaction, we need to add the effects of increased immigration, whether in the form of skilled and professional economic migrants or unskilled legal and illegal workers, and a rise in what has been perceived as a 'refugee crisis' as poorer nation states have either imploded, partly as a result of disastrous Western interventions, or have simply not developed quickly enough to feed their growing populations.

Many refugees have made hazardous journeys to reach European shores and America's southern border to escape civil war and poverty, creating fertile soil for what have been called 'nativist' backlashes. Islamic terrorism, although committed by a minority of Muslims, whether home-grown or from abroad, has created an extraordinary securitization of the state apparatuses of Western nations which have made whole Muslim populations in Europe and the USA easy targets for fear, demonization, and further racialization, as I explored in the section on Islamophobia in Chapter 4.

These trends have led to a mushrooming of support for right-wing radical parties and the creation of new ones. This is a phenomenon that has generally been characterized by the idea that what the world as a whole has experienced is the growth of right-wing 'populism', for the phenomenon is by no means confined to the West: the Philippines, Brazil, Turkey, India, and to some extent Australia, to take just some illustrations, have seen the rise of their own versions. Of course, there have been left-wing versions too, in the form of Podemos in Spain, the Occupy Wall Street movement, Bernie Sanders's campaign for democratic socialism in the USA, and the tremendous growth of youth support for the British Labour Party, which has coalesced around a movement that has called itself 'Momentum'.

In my analysis in this concluding chapter, however, I am going to focus mainly on right-wing radical populist parties, for they carry the greatest threat that race and racism, far from being of diminishing importance, will be more important racializing drivers of the politics of Europe and the USA in the coming decades.

Debating the concept of 'populism'

Scholars of the continuing growth of right-wing radical parties are by no means agreed that 'populism' is the most appropriate form of conceptualization for describing and analysing these movements and parties. Nevertheless, there seems to be a growing consensus among both scholars and those involved in broader public debates that 'populism', for want of a more adequate concept, does indeed provide a suitable initial framework for understanding these right-wing movements and parties and their ideologies.

In its simplest form, the notion of populism grasps that populist movements present a critique of the establishment and the status quo by pitting the 'pure people' against 'the corrupt elite', as

Mudde and Kaltwasser put it. This is obviously a *moral* argument, but it is a 'thin' ideological framework, for it does not specify exactly who the protagonists are. The people and the elite are *constructed* by movements, and their composition will be influenced by a huge variety of factors, depending on the historical specificity of the circumstances that allow these movements to present themselves as the authentic voice or will of the people who have allegedly been betrayed by the corrupt elite.

Populism is therefore inevitably what Molyneux and Osborne have called a 'hybrid', for it has to draw upon a variety of salient ideological elements to construct a perspective in which the people can recognize themselves as such, and they may be constrained by the institutional complex within which the politics of the nation are carried out. For example, where there are relatively robust national liberal democratic institutions, the populists have to temper their ideology so that it does not violate democratic norms too openly, and this may require a process of 'detoxification' and a slight or larger movement to the centre ground; the evolution of the Front National (now National Rally) in France under Marine Le Pen is one such example, where antisemitism has been played down (albeit by substituting it with a more popular Islamophobia), while street violence is also discouraged. On the other hand, where the hold of liberal democratic institutions is weak, as in Hungary, Viktor Orbán has been openly proclaiming the need for and moving towards an 'illiberal democracy', which has fewer vestiges of pluralist institutions like freedom of political association for the opposition, and restrictions placed on the expression of opposition voices in the press. Institutions such as universities are also placed under scrutiny and intimidated so that opposition to the ruling party is muted. Moreover, Orbán has created a fertile space for open antisemitism, playing upon longstanding cultural currents.

There are other general aspects of populism that are worth noting. They tend towards a cult of the leader, leaving them vulnerable if the leader dies or is seriously compromised in some way. Thus, many such movements are short-lived. By the same token, the leadership cult can lead to authoritarianism and a temptation for the leader to declare herself or himself the personification of the 'people's will'. Moreover, while left-wing versions generally have a simpler version of the 'pure people' against a corrupt elite, right-wing versions tend to invoke a third element that can act as a scapegoat: immigrants and other minorities tend to be favourite targets, portrayed as parasitic upon hard-working natives, for example in the form of getting undeserved welfare handouts, and the reviled elite is accused of colluding actively with these parasitic others against the interests of the more deserving authentic 'people'. In other versions, the elite is accused of being too liberal towards gays, lesbians, feminists, and others who betray 'family values'. In such cases the elite is painted as 'metropolitan' or too 'cosmopolitan' (the latter of course has a long history as an antisemitic trope as well).

Right-wing populism is more often than not a politics of fear, with warnings of an enemy within. It is also a politics of resentment and anger. It allows a release of longstanding, pent-up emotions and frustrations, building upon and mobilizing sentiments that elites have for too long not paid enough attention to the people's voice. Thus, populists are apt to invoke the idea of the 'silent majority', a phrase effectively used by President Richard Nixon and thereafter invoked again in the USA, and in the UK and other European nation states. The notion of an ignored 'moral majority' is another that is often invoked by right-wing populists. Finally, populists have a tendency to propose simplistic solutions to complex problems, and this is where scapegoats provide a handy substitute for serious policy programmes: if only immigration was curtailed, or if only transnational organizations such as the European Union were dumped, 'the people's problems' would be well on their way to being solved.

Right-wing populism: a brief, selective survey of Europe in 2019

In France, the Front National won 13 per cent of the vote in national elections and has eight seats in the National Assembly, and Marine Le Pen was the runner up in the presidential race. In Austria the Freedom Party won 26 per cent of the national vote and is now in a coalition government with the Austrian People's Party which has itself shifted to the right under pressure. Germany has the Alternative for Germany party at 12.6 per cent of the vote and a parliamentary representation of ninety-four seats in the Bundestag. In Switzerland the Swiss People's Party is the largest party in the Federal Parliament with sixty-five members, while in the Netherlands the Party for Freedom has gained twenty seats and is the second largest parliamentary party. The Danish People's Party won 21 per cent of the vote in the 2015 general election, but in the European elections increased its vote share to 27 per cent. The Swedish Democrats won 62 parliamentary seats with over 17 per cent of the vote. The Finns Party (previously known as the True Finns) won 18 per cent of the national vote. Fidesz in Hungary has 133 out of 199 seats, Golden Dawn in Greece won 7 per cent of the national vote, and in Italy, at the time of writing, there is a governing coalition between The League and Beppe Grillo's Five Star movement. The Norwegian Progress Party is the third largest and is part of the centre-right coalition government.

These parties are not all cut from the same political cloth. Some, like the Norwegian Progress Party, have libertarian, low-tax, small government programmes, while others, like the Danish People's Party, are very pro-welfare, but only for whoever is regarded as genuinely a native or longstanding citizen. The right-wing populists also have varying policies towards globalization and the European Union.

Even this synoptic survey shows that in the last twelve years since the first edition of this book was published, the populist right has been on the march in Europe, west and east, and is unlikely to disappear soon. On the contrary, it is likely to stabilize and probably increase in political and cultural significance.

'The four Ds'

Given the heterogeneity of the policies and politics of populist right-wing radicalism, is it possible to have a broad explanatory framework which can encompass them all? And which can also include Brexit and the Trump phenomena?

Roger Eatwell and Mathew Goodwin have proposed just such an explanatory schema, which they encapsulate in the formula 'the four Ds'. While it has its flaws, this framework is useful, and especially so because it proposes an assessment of *the degree of racism* entailed by the rise of what they call (right-wing) 'National Populism'. The four Ds refer to distrust of power elites, destruction of national culture and identity, relative deprivation, and dealignment between electorates and mainstream parties.

I will argue that although their explanation of what they call national populism has its merits, their understanding of racism is deeply flawed. It exhibits all the faults of the particular understanding of racism that I have been arguing *against*, and therefore allows me to show why the form of analysis I have been arguing for is to be preferred in understanding the future of racism given the context of the rise of right-wing radicalism or 'national populism' in Europe and the USA.

Eatwell and Goodwin emphasize, rightly, that the spurt in the growth of national populist parties needs to be understood in the context of a longer history than the great recession of 2008 or recent social panics over refugees. The Austrian Freedom Party has its origins in the late 1950s, and the French Front National, to take another illustration, was founded in 1972. Some of these parties have fascist roots, the Swedish Democrats and the National Front being classic examples. Nevertheless, the period since the 1990s has seen a spectacular growth in the number of national populist parties and their electoral support, and previously fascist beginnings have been set aside, sometimes simply for opportunist, electoral advantage. According to Eatwell and Goodwin, this growth in radical right-wing national populism has occurred because of an intensification of the four Ds.

The first D refers to a growing *distrust* of the power and integrity of the elites who increasingly dominate politics in liberal democracies. The elites are more and more drawn from a small proportion of the middle and upper classes (in the UK, for example, privately schooled and Oxbridge educated, in France graduates of the *grandes écoles*). Fewer seem to have had any experience outside of politics. This is part of the professionalization of politics and the rise of what Peter Oborne has called 'the triumph of the political class'. Alternatively, or in addition, the political elites are considerably wealthier than the majority of the electorate (many cabinets in Western governments contain a disproportionate share of millionaires). In the USA the cost of getting elected to public office makes the political class beholden to wealthy special interests who are able to donate, lobby, and get special access, while the general evisceration of trade unions and the marginalization of civic organizations has meant that ordinary citizens feel disempowered. In countries like Spain and Greece there has been endemic and well-known corruption among the political and business elites that has also eroded trust, while in the UK the expenses scandal involving MPs contributed to the already growing belief that politicians of all stripes 'are the same' and only 'in it for themselves'. The growing similarity between formerly left social democrats, in thrall to pro-market, neoliberal policies, and the centre-right has added to the sense that ordinary citizens have a narrow choice of policies, most of which favour the wealthy (lower taxes, privatization of formerly publicly owned services, the power of shareholders and their desire for short-term gain, the power and greed exhibited by banks which led to the recession of 2008 and its aftermath of austerity for local public bodies while the bonus culture of bankers continued to thrive, and so forth).

The second 'D' is provocatively labelled *destruction* by Eatwell and Goodwin, and refers to the growing fear among ordinary citizens that immigration and rapid ethnic change is leading to the death of a cherished national identity and familiar cultural markers. The idea that we feel like 'strangers in our own country', as the title of Arlie Hochschild's book puts it, is a cry that is often heard and seized upon by populist nationalists. Nigel Farage, now leader of the fast-rising Brexit Party, once complained that on a train journey he felt awkward when he heard no English being spoken, a remark that summed up the often-felt helplessness in the face of globalization, immigration, and 'ethnic churn' that the British, and especially the English, have been resenting, especially since the arrival of Poles, Hungarians, and others from eastern Europe since 2004.

Again, the sense is that while cheap labour is good for employers and those who can afford nannies and gardeners, as well as private health care and education and a cosmopolitan, globalized lifestyle, the 'silent majority' has felt the effects of strained public services, the decline of familiar local life and manners, and declining living standards and job prospects. Anger and resentment are particularly potent results of the fears generated by the decline in traditional national identities, forces which mainstream parties, with their commitment to reasoned debate and opposition to demagoguery, are especially poorly placed to mobilize. In this context, as in others, historically specific drivers will always be in play. Dorling and Tomlinson make a compelling case that for the English in particular, the loss of empire has been a grievous blow which has left them nostalgic for regaining greatness and a leading global role, rather than being relatively small players in a co-operative venture with former enemies like Germany and France who are now dominant in the European Union. Note, in this context, that Northern Ireland and Scotland voted to stay in the EU (although Wales voted by a very small majority to leave). Brexit found its largest support in England.

The third, related 'D' refers to the *relative deprivation* felt by the majority in which a small proportion of the population continues to grab very large rewards in unequal societies. In many Western countries the slogan of the 1 per cent against the 99 per cent resonated with large sections of society, especially the young, who feel that the security and prosperity enjoyed by their parents is disappearing, to be replaced by a form of precarity in work as well as other spheres such as housing, as employers have greater power in the labour market and cuts in public services, for example in the UK, have led to a shrinking social housing stock, loss of publicly funded local amenities like libraries, youth clubs, children's nurseries, and so forth.

The term 'relative' is important here. Many of the supporters of national populism, such as Trump's electoral base, are not drawn from the poorest section of society who either tend not to vote or vote for Democrats in the USA and social democratic parties in Europe. National populism finds some of its strongest support among those with jobs and average or median earnings, but also among relatively well-off pensioners who have very little social contact with immigrants, and employers, for whom national populism provides an opportunity to advance a neoliberal agenda of low taxation, a shrinking state, deregulation of standards of health and safety protections at work, and an easier environment for hiring and sacking workers.

The final 'D' refers to *dealignment*, that is, the growing volatility of support for and declining membership of mainstream parties. Social democratic parties in western Europe have found themselves at the sharp end, as right-wing national populists have increasingly espoused the cause of the working class and the 'left behind', who feel their concerns have gone unheeded by social democratic cosmopolitan elites. However, it is important to note that the anti-immigrant sentiments and voting patterns of the working classes in particular have pushed all mainstream political parties, including formerly liberal social democrats, into becoming tough on immigration control as well as tending more generally towards the illiberal right of politics, especially in the form of abandoning attempts at multiculturalism and stressing the need for immigrants and their offspring to 'integrate' into national and, in the case of Muslims, more broadly defined 'Western' values.

Level of education has emerged as a key dividing line between supporters of national populism and those, especially the degree-level educated, who feel more comfortable in the new multiethnic, cosmopolitan, globalized world. Those with fewer educational qualifications are much more likely to support national populism.

Also, many commentators on right-wing populism argue that in actuality populism blurs the left–right distinction, for it attracts support from a wide range of voters, and that the policies they advocate, especially in relation to paying more attention to the concerns of the working classes, formerly more likely to be part of a left-wing or social democratic platform, are now championed by right-wing national populists.

National populism and the future of racism

Eatwell and Goodwin admit that 'there is absolutely no doubt that some national populists veer into racism and xenophobia, especially towards Muslims'. But, they argue, the majority of supporters are not racists and that accusations of racism anger these supporters.

However, Eatwell and Goodwin have a narrow, restrictive definition of racism which completely misunderstands its complexity and nuance, and especially its connections with notions of 'the nation' and, in the case of the English, a nostalgia for the days of empire. They create a binary division between those who are definitely racists (said by them to be a minority) and non-racists (the majority). In their conceptual terminology this is presented as a differentiation between 'blatant racists' of the 'old style', who believe in 'a hierarchic and antagonistic' characterization of populations. There is a nod towards 'cultural racism', but this term is discounted in their analysis, as are 'institutional racism' and 'implicit bias'. The reason they give for rejecting these concepts is that their deployment would encompass *large numbers of white people and social institutions as "racist"'* (my emphasis), a charge which 'clearly alienates and even angers people. They can stifle important debates around immigration and Islam.'

This is a striking admission. In other words, if we follow the framework recommended in my book, and take notions like cultural racism, institutional (and structural) racism, and Islamophobia (a term that appears in their 332-page book only once, in a direct quotation from the former British prime minister, David Cameron) seriously, large numbers of white people would be caught up in the net of racism. It is because they fail to understand notions such as racialization, the idea that the notion of 'nation' is closely linked to 'race', that in popular discourse 'race–nation–ethnicity' operates as a complex triad in which each slides repeatedly and inconsistently into the other, that cultural racism, and institutional and structural racisms, are real forms of racism, and that hostility to Islam can become a form of bio-cultural racism (as I showed earlier), that they are able to maintain a strict distinction between 'national populism' and racism.

By the same token, they grossly underestimate the degree to which racism exists in Europe and the USA. Put differently, if my analysis of racism is accepted, then *by their own admission* these societies are thoroughly racialized, and many of those angered by the charge of racism against themselves would have to re-evaluate their self-understanding as well as their collusion in racist thinking and practices.

Support for my argument (and the unwitting views of Eatwell and Goodwin) comes from an exhaustive study of racial attitudes undertaken by Flemmen and Savage, based on an examination of a wide range of research, including the British National Child Development Study which has followed a group of children born in 1958. Their analysis reveals that possibly a large majority of the British population have 'ambivalent' or 'weak anti-racist views' which have 'the potential to be mobilized in racist directions'. It is arguable that this is precisely what partly explains the Leave vote in the Brexit referendum, especially given that the Leave campaign played upon the anti-immigrant sentiment that was displayed by a large proportion of Leave voters, both during the campaign and since.

Eatwell and Goodwin are joined by those, like Kaufman, who make an unconvincing distinction between 'racial self-interest' and racism, and David Goodhart who argues that a defence of whiteness is not racist. For one thing, this ignores facts about structural racism which create in-built advantages for white people in white-dominated societies. Moreover, white and black are both racialized categories, which is why in this book I have devoted large sections to discussing them. It makes no sense to suggest that they can be stripped of their racial connotations and treated in some racially neutral manner. Moreover, as Miri Song has argued, there is not a 'racial equivalence' between what seem like racist acts on the part of ethnic minorities (and by implication the defence of black self-interest), and white racist acts and 'racial' self-interest: in a white-dominated society in which ethnic minorities are severely disadvantaged, acting to preserve white self-interest is to act in support of a status quo that systematically discriminates against ethnic minorities. As Bhambra puts it: 'The difference between minorities and majorities expressing group sentiments is that the sentiments of the former arise in the context of a wish for *inclusion* and *equality*, while those of the latter are a consequence of a wish to *exclude* and to *dominate*' (emphasis in original).

The term 'nativism', popular in the political science literature on populism, also strips the underlying sentiments of racialization, for 'nativism' in white-dominated societies is used in a manner that denies genuine belonging to ethnic minorities. Authentic natives are 'white' citizens in this discourse. The notion that nativism is a non-racial concept is highly implausible: it exists in a spectrum of continuity within what I have called the 'race–nation–ethnicity' complex.

I have some sympathy for Eatwell, Goodwin, Kaufman, and Goodhart in so far as they make the argument that mainstream politics has left the less educated, 'just managing' parts of the population in Europe and the USA unheard. But these parts of population most definitely include ethnic minorities, and indeed the evidence I have presented shows that ethnic minorities suffer, and have historically suffered, much greater disadvantage than their white counterparts. In this sense, Eatwell and Goodwin are guilty of what Bhambra has labelled 'methodological whiteness' (her remarks are also directed at the American researcher Arlie Hochschild, whose *Strangers in Their Own Land* also underplays the disadvantaged position of blacks and Hispanics).

Eatwell and Goodwin end their book with some suggestions for a 'post-populist' future. Tackling racial disadvantage, *except for that which is perceived by whites as being perpetrated against them* (what has come to be labelled 'reverse racism' and which I discussed in Chapter 5), does not enter the frame. They advance a curious idea that the working class is 'instinctively conservative' and liberal elites would do well to temper their liberalism when it comes to anti-racism, multiculturalism, support for gay rights, feminism, and so forth. But they provide no reasons for the argument that working-class conservatism is somehow 'instinctive' (thus also wiping out two centuries of working-class radicalism). What exactly is meant by 'instinct'? Eatwell and Goodwin beg this rather important question.

A more plausible explanation is that, sociologically speaking, many sections of the working class increasingly occupy insecure jobs: factory relocations, temporary work, and 'zero-hour' contracts at or below the minimum wage are on the rise. A fear of further rapid change in values towards liberalism, including liberal immigration policies which result in the loss of familiar cultural landmarks, heightens this insecurity, especially when they happen in combination with pressure on public services. It is then easy to mobilize resentments against immigrants or the EU, rather than the neoliberal policies of national governments that have deliberately imposed austerity, and a shrinkage in resources available to local authorities. We are not just in the midst of some abstract 'culture clash' between liberal and conservative values which is fuelling racism and 'national populism', or between respect for authority and a more liberal approach (this is Kaufman's argument), although both are clearly involved.

One factor, however, that may have driven the male vote to Leave (and Trump's support from men) is the degree of women's entry into the labour force and a focus on women's aspirations for equality, according to research undertaken by Gidron and Hall. To put it differently, a perceived threat to masculinity in an era of declining opportunities for men, especially in older industries, may be said to have played a part too.

Dorling and Tomlinson make a compelling case in *Rule Britannia: Brexit and the End of Empire* that the success of the

Leave campaign in the UK referendum on Brexit relied decisively on middle-class voters in 'Middle England', especially older voters who had been brought up on a diet of school books that glorified the British Empire and a sense that Britain had 'stood alone' and won World War II, thus giving them confidence that they could go it alone again. 'All across the UK, some 60 per cent of all those voting Brexit [that is, "Leave"] were aged over sixty and had mostly started school between 1930 and 1960.' This was a generation that was brought up to feel superior not only to colonials, but to all foreigners. An imperial mindset among older middle-class voters is also noticed in the research by Flemmen and Savage.

As far as the working-class vote is concerned, Dorling and Tomlinson confirm the analysis of relative deprivation: 'It was not the poor voters but the averagely off voters who *felt* poor that mattered most' (emphasis in original). As they point out, there is no evidence that the poorer the area, the more likely its residents were to vote Leave.

But Eatwell, Goodwin, Kaufman, and Goodhart, and those who agree with them, also need to take the argument of my book seriously. Structural and ideological racisms are strongly embedded in the white-majority societies of Europe and the USA. Right-wing national populism, to the extent that it legitimately articulates the voices of the 'left behind', is also part of a rise in racism and xenophobia which has been given a public space and voice in national politics. To ignore it is to leave its rise unchecked.

It is noteworthy that Eatwell and Goodwin ignore the fact that the spate of hate crimes spiked after the Brexit referendum and the election of Trump. The murder of the MP Jo Cox goes unmentioned, as does the Trump family's alleged long history of racial discrimination against potential black tenants (note that this discrimination has been denied by the Trump family) and Trump's view that in a neo-Nazi march that was met with an organized protest 'there were fine people on both sides'. The idea that neo-Nazis contain 'fine people' sits ill with Eatwell and Goodwin's view that Trump is definitely not a 'white supremacist'. A reading of Churchwell's *Behold America: A History of America First and the American Dream* would disabuse them of the notion that 'America First' and 'Make America Great Again' are not also part of a dog-whistle politics that appeals to white racism.

Eatwell and Goodwin are correct in their judgement that national populism is here to stay. By the same token—and this is what they fail to recognize—so is racism, and now even more so in the wake of the successes of national populism.

It is particularly worrying, as Stocker, Wendling, and others have argued, that the so-called 'alt-right' and the extreme right have been emboldened by the successes of Brexit, Trump, and other populisms. There is a great danger that many sections of what Goodhart calls 'decent populists' and the far right will coalesce, perhaps in unstable configurations, especially via the new social media, into a far more dangerous right-wing form of racism. It is no wonder that authors like Enzo Traverso are now beginning to talk of *The New Faces of Fascism*. There is every possibility that the present normalization of xenophobia, 'nativism', populist nationalism, and racism in white-dominated societies will combine with authoritarianism to form a 'new normal' which will entrench and extend the reach of racism even further.

No scholar of racism can contemplate the future with complacency or optimism.

References

Chapter 2. Imperialism, genocide, and the 'science' of race

Z. Bauman, *Modernity and the Holocaust* (Cambridge: Polity Press, 1989).

W. Dalrymple, *White Moghuls: Love and Betrayal in 18th Century India* (London: Harper, 2004).

E. Katz, *Confronting Evil* (Albany: State University of New York Press, 2004).

A. Nandy, *Intimate Enemy: Loss and Recovery of Self Under Colonialism* (Oxford: Oxford University Press, 1983).

N. Ohler, *Blitzed: Drugs in Nazi Germany* (London: Allen Lane, 2016).

A. Rattansi, *Bauman and Contemporary Sociology: A Critical Analysis* (Manchester: Manchester University Press, 2017).

E. Said, *Orientalism* (London: Allen Lane, 1978).

Chapter 3. The demise of scientific racism

K. Carrico, *The Great Han: Race, Nationalism and Tradition in China Today* (Oakland: University of California Press, 2017).

R. Lewontin, 'The apportionment of human diversity', *Evolutionary Biology* 6 (1972): 391–8.

M. Meloni, *Political Biology: Science and Social Values in Human Heredity from Eugenics to Epigenetics* (London: Palgrave Macmillan, 2016).

A. Morning, *The Nature of Race: How Scientists Think and Teach About Human Difference* (Oakland: University of California Press, 2011).

A. Morning, 'And you thought we had moved beyond all that: biological race returns to the social sciences', *Ethnic and Racial Studies* 37 (10) (2014): 1676–85.

D. Reich, *Who We Are and How We Got Here: Ancient DNA and the New Science of the Human Past* (Oxford: Oxford University Press, 2018).

A. Saini, *Superior: The Return of Race Science* (London: Fourth Estate, 2019).

N. Wade, *A Troublesome Inheritance: Genes, Race and Human History* (New York: Penguin, 2016).

Chapter 4. Racialization, cultural racism, and religion

M. Billig, *Banal Nationalism* (London: Sage, 1995).

J. Carr, *Experiences of Islamophobia: Living with Racism in the Neo-liberal Era* (Abingdon: Routledge, 2016).

J. Dixon and M. Levine, *Beyond Prejudice: Extending the Social Psychology of Conflict, Inequality and Social Change* (Cambridge: Cambridge University Press, 2012).

R. Fine and P. Spencer, *Antisemitism and the Left: On the Return of the Jewish Question* (Manchester: Manchester University Press, 2017).

F. Halliday, 'Islamophobia reconsidered', *Ethnic and Racial Studies* 22 (5) (1999): 892–902.

D. Hirsch, *Contemporary Left Antisemitism* (Abingdon: Routledge, 2017).

S. Huntington, *The Clash of Civilizations* (New York: Simon and Schuster, 1997).

A. Hussey, *The French Intifada: The Long War between France and its Arabs* (London: Granta, 2014).

J. Karabel, *The Chosen: The Hidden History of Admission and Exclusion at Harvard, Yale, and Princeton* (New York: Mariner Books, 2006).

B. Klug, 'The collective Jew: Israel and the new antisemitism', *Patterns of Prejudice* 37 (2) (2003): 1–19.

B. Klug, 'The myth of a new antisemitism', *The Nation*, 15 January: 7.

B. Klug, 'Islamophobia: a concept comes of age', *Ethnicities* 12 (5) (2012): 665–81.

N. Lean, *The Islamophobia Industry: How the Right Manufactures Fear of Muslims* (London: Pluto Press, 2012).

E. Love, *Islamophobia and Racism in America* (New York: New York University Press, 2017).

M. Mack, *Sexagon: Muslims, France and the Sexualization of National Culture* (New York: Fordham University Press, 2017).

N. Massoumi, T. Mills, and D. Miller, *What is Islamophobia? Racism, Social Movements and the State* (London: Pluto Press 2017).

P. Morey and A. Yaqim, *Framing Muslims: Stereotyping and Representation after 9/11* (Cambridge, MA: Harvard University Press, 2011).

A. Morning, *The Nature of Race: How Scientists Think and Teach about Human Difference* (Oakland: University of California Press, 2011).

M. Omi and H. Winant, *Racial Formation in the United States*, 3rd edition (New York: Routledge, 2015).

J. Petley and R. Richardson, *Pointing the Finger: Islam and Muslims in the British Media* (Oxford: Oneworld, 2011).

A. Rattansi, 'The uses of racialization: space, time and the raced body', in K. Murji and J. Solomos (eds), *Racialization: Studies in Theory and Practice* (Oxford: Oxford University Press, 2005).

K. Sian, I. Law, and S. Sayyid, *Racism, Governance and Public Policy: Beyond Human Rights* (Abingdon: Routledge, 2013).

P. Silverstein, *Postcolonial France: Race, Islam and the Future of the Republic* (London: Pluto Press, 2018).

S. Tharoor, *Inglorious Empire: What the British Did to India* (London: Allen Lane, 2016).

D. Tyrer, *The Politics of Islamophobia: Race, Power and Fantasy* (London: Pluto Press, 2013).

Chapter 5. Structural racism and colourblind whiteness

M. Alexander, *The New Jim Crow* (New York: The New Press, 2012).

E. Bonilla-Silva, *Colour-Blind Racism and the Persistence of Racial Inequality in America*, 5th edition (Lanham: Rowman and Littlefield, 2018).

M. Brown, M. Carnoy, E. Currie, T. Duster, D. Oppenheimer, M. Schultz, and D. Wellman, *Whitewashing Race: The Myth of a Colour-blind Society* (Oakland: University of California Press, 2003).

M. Burke, *Colourblind Racism* (Cambridge: Polity Press, 2019).

T.-N. Coates, *We Were Eight Years in Power: An American Tragedy* (London: Hamish Hamilton, 2017).

R. Diangelo, *White Fragility: Why It's So Hard for White People to Talk about Race* (Boston: Beacon Press, 2018).

R. Eddo-Lodge, *Why I'm No Longer Talking to White People about Race* (London: Bloomsbury, 2017).

J. Forman, *Locking Up Our Own: Crime and Punishment in Black America* (London: Abacus, 2018).

R. Frankenburg, *White Women, Race Matters* (Madison: University of Wisconsin Press, 1994).

S. Garner, *Racisms*, 2nd edition (London: Sage, 2017).

E. Glenn (ed.), *Shades of Difference: Why Skin Colour Matters* (Stanford: Stanford University Press, 2009).

A. Hacker, *Two Nations: Black and White, Separate, Hostile, Unequal* (New York: Ballantine Books, 1992).

R. Hohle, *Racism in the Neoliberal Era: A Meta History of White Power* (New York: Routledge, 2018).

M. Hunter, *Race, Gender, and the Politics of Skin Tone* (Abingdon: Taylor and Francis, 2005).

P. Ioanide, *The Emotional Politics of Racism: How Feelings Trump Facts in an Era of Colourblindness* (Stanford: Stanford University Press, 2015).

G. Lipsitz, *The Possessive Investment in Whiteness: How White People Profit from Identity Politics*, revised edition (Philadelphia: Temple University Press, 2006).

I. Lopez, *Dog Whistle Politics: How Coded Racial Appeals Have Reinvented Racism and Wrecked the Middle Classes* (Oxford: Oxford University Press, 2014).

D. Massey and N. Denton, *American Apartheid: Segregation and the Making of an Underclass* (Cambridge, MA: Harvard University Press, 1993).

K. Murji, *Racism, Policy and Politics* (Bristol: Policy Press, 2017).

C. Ogletree, *The Presumption of Guilt: The Arrest of Henry Louis Gates Jr., and Race, Class and Crime in America* (New York: Palgrave Macmillan, 2010).

A. Phoenix, 'I'm white—so what? The construction of whiteness for young Londoners', in M. Fine (ed.), *Off White* (New York: Routledge, 1996).

A. Phoenix, 'Remembered racializations: young people and positioning in different understandings', in K. Murji and J. Solomos (eds), *Racialization: Studies in Theory and Practice* (Oxford: Oxford University Press, 2005).

D. Roithmayr, *Reproducing Racism: How Everyday Choices Lock In White Advantage* (New York: New York University Press, 2014).

R. Shilliam, *Race and the Undeserving Poor* (Newcastle upon Tyne: Agenda Publishing, 2018).

M. Song, 'Challenging a culture of racial equivalence', *The British Journal of Sociology* 65 (1) (2014): 108–29.

S. Tharoor, *Inglorious Empire: What the British Did to India* (London: Allen Lane, 2016).

B. Trepagnier, *Silent Racism: How Well-meaning White People Perpetuate the Racial Divide*, 2nd edition (Abingdon: Routledge, 2016).

K. Tyler, 'The racialized and classed constitution of village life in Leicestershire', *Ethnos* 68 (3) (2005): 391–42.

P. Wachtel, *Race in the Mind of America* (London: Routledge, 1999).

C. West, 'Pity the sad legacy of Barack Obama', *The Guardian*, 9 January 2017.

T. Wise, *Colourblind: Barack Obama, Post-Racial Liberalism and the Retreat from Racial Equity* (San Francisco: City Lights Publishers, 2010).

Chapter 6. Intersectionality and 'implicit' or 'unconscious' bias

M. Banaji and A. Greenwald, *Blindspot: Hidden Biases of Good People* (New York: Bantam, 2016).

P. Collins and S. Bilge, *Intersectionality* (Cambridge: Polity Press, 2016).

K. Crenshaw, *On Intersectionality: Essential Writings* (New York: New Press, 2020).

P. Essed, *Understanding Everyday Racism* (London: Sage 1991).

A. Hirsch, *Brit(ish): On Race, Identity and Belonging* (London: Jonathan Cape, 2018).

A. Hirsch, 'This is a vital study of racial bias: now will Britain take heed?', *The Guardian*, 2 Deccmber 2018. https://www.theguardian.com/commentisfree/2018/dec/02/bias-in-britain-racial-bias-ethnic-minorities.

J. Kahn, *Race on the Brain: What Implicit Bias Gets Wrong About the Struggle for Racial Justice* (New York: Columbia University Press, 2018).

D. Kahneman, *Thinking Fast and Slow* (London: Penguin, 2012).

M. Romero, *Introducing Intersectionality* (Cambridge: Polity Press, 2018).

N. Shukla (ed.), *The Good Immigrant* (London: Unbound Books, 2017).

A. Smith, *Racism and Everyday Life* (London: Palgrave Macmillan, 2015).

Chapter 7. The rise of right-wing national populism and the future of racism

A. Banks, *Anger and Racial Politics: The Emotional Foundation of Racial Attitudes in America* (Cambridge: Cambridge University Press, 2014).

M. Benjamin, *The Global Rise of Populism: Performance, Political Style and Representation* (Stanford: Stanford University Press, 2016).

G. Bhambra, 'Brexit, Trump and "methodological whiteness": on the misrecognition of race and class', *The British Journal of Sociology* 68 (S1) (2017): 215–32.

L. Bobo, 'Racism in Trump's America: reflections on culture, sociology, and the 2016 presidential election', *The British Journal of Sociology* 68 (S1) (2017): 85–104.

S. Churchwell, *Behold America: A History of America First and the American Dream* (London: Bloomsbury, 2018).

D. Dorling and S. Tomlinson, *Rule Britannia: Brexit and the End of Empire* (London: Biteback Publishing, 2019).

R. Eatwell and M. Goodwin, *National Populism: The Revolt Against Liberal Democracy* (London: Penguin, 2018).

M. Flemman and M. Savage, 'The politics of nationalism and white racism in the UK', *The British Journal of Sociology* 68 (S1) (2017): 233–64.

N. Gidron and P. Hall, 'The politics of social status: economic and cultural roots of the populist right', *The British Journal of Sociology* 68 (S1) (2017): 58–84.

D. Goodhart, *The Road to Somewhere: The Populist Revolt and the Future of Politics* (London: Hurst, 2017).

A. Hochschild, *Strangers in Their Own Land: Anger and Mourning on the American Right* (New York: The New Press 2016).

P. Ioanide, *The Emotional Politics of Racism: How Feelings Trump Facts in an Era of Colour-blindness* (Stanford: Stanford University Press, 2015).

E. Kaufman, *Whiteshift: Populism, Immigration and the Future of White Majorities* (London: Allen Lane, 2018).

M. Molyneux and T. Osborne, 'Populism: a deflationary view', *Economy and Society* 46 (1) (2017): 1–19.

C. Mudde and C. Kaltwasser, *Populism: A Very Short Introduction* (Oxford: Oxford University Press, 2017).

P. Oborne, *The Triumph of the Political Class*, revised edition (London: Pocket Books 2007).

T. Skocpol and V. Williams, *The Tea Party and the Remaking of Republican Conservatism*, 2nd edition (Oxford: Oxford University Press, 2016).

M. Song, 'Challenging a culture of racial equivalence', *British Journal of Sociology* 65 (1) (2014): 107–29.

P. Stocker, *English Uprising: Brexit and the Mainstreaming of the Far Right* (London: Melville House, 2017).

E. Traverso, *The New Faces of Fascism: Populism and the Far Right* (London: Verso, 2019).

M. Wendling, *Alt-Right: From 4chan to the White House* (London: Pluto Press 2018).

Further reading

Chapter 1. 'Race' and racism: some conundrums

B. Isaac, *The Invention of Racism in Classical Antiquity* (Princeton: Princeton University Press, 2004).

A. Lindemann, *Antisemitism Before the Holocaust* (London: Longman, 2000).

W. Lowery, *They Can't Kill Us All: The Story of Black Lives Matter* (London: Penguin, 2017).

M. Taibbi, *I Can't Breathe: The Killing that Started a Movement* (London: W. H. Allen, 2018).

Chapter 2. Imperialism, genocide, and the 'science' of race

M. Banton, *Racial Theories*, 2nd edition (Cambridge: Cambridge University Press, 1998).

D. Bindman, *Ape to Apollo: Aesthetics and the Idea of Race in the Eighteenth Century* (London: Reaktion Books, 2002).

B. Cohn, *Colonialism and Its Forms of Knowledge* (Princeton: Princeton University Press, 1996).

N. Dirks, *Castes of Mind: Colonialism and the Making of Modern India* (Princeton: Princeton University Press, 2011).

A. Gill, *Ruling Passions: Sex, Race and Empire* (London: BBC Books, 1995).

S. Gilman, 'Black bodies, white bodies: towards an iconography of female sexuality in late nineteenth century art, medicine and literature', in J. Donald and A. Rattansi (eds), *'Race', Culture and Difference* (London: Sage, 1992).

S. Hall, 'The West and the rest', in S. Hall and B. Gieben (eds),
Formations of Modernity (Cambridge: Polity Press, 1992).

B. Isaac, *The Invention of Racism in Classical Antiquity* (Princeton:
Princeton University Press, 2004).

I. Kershaw, *Hitler, the Germans and the Final Solution* (New Haven:
Yale University Press, 2009).

J. MacKenzie, *Orientalism: History, Theory and the Arts* (Manchester:
Manchester University Press, 2011).

A. McLintock, *Imperial Leather: Race, Gender and Sexuality in the
Colonial Contest* (London: Routledge, 1995).

M. Mann, *The Dark Side of Democracy: Explaining Ethnic Cleansing*
(Cambridge: Cambridge University Press, 2005).

P. Robb (ed.), *The Concept of Race in South Asia* (Oxford: Oxford
University Press, 1995).

D. Stone, *The Historiography of the Holocaust* (Basingstoke: Palgrave
Macmillan, 2004).

J. Walvin, *Black Ivory: Slavery in the British Empire*, 2nd edition
(Oxford: Blackwell, 2001).

Chapter 3. The demise of scientific racism

A. Alland, *Race in Mind: Race, IQ and Other Racisms* (Basingstoke:
Palgrave Macmillan, 2002).

E. Barkan, *The Retreat of Scientific Racism* (Cambridge: Cambridge
University Press, 1993).

S. Gould, *The Mismeasure of Man*, 2nd edition (New York: Norton, 1996).

R. Lewontin, 'Are the races different?', *Science for the People* 14 (2)
(1982): 10–14.

Chapter 4. Racialization, cultural racism, and religion

E. Balibar, 'Is there a neo-racism?', in E. Balibar and I. Wallerstein
(eds), *Race, Nation and Class* (London: Verso, 1991).

M. Barker, *The New Racism* (London: Junction Books, 1982).

Chapter 5. Structural racism and colourblind whiteness

P. Cohen, 'Labouring Under Whiteness', in R. Frankenber (ed.),
Displacing Whiteness (Durham, NC: Duke University Press, 1997).

S. Garner, *Whiteness: An Introduction* (Abingdon: Routledge, 2007).

I. Ignatiev, *How the Irish Became White* (New York: Routledge, 1995).

M. Jacobsen, *Whiteness of a Different Colour: European Immigrants and the Alchemy of Race* (Cambridge, MA: Harvard University Press, 1998).

T. Wise, *White Like Me: Reflections on Race from a Privileged Son*, revised edition (Berkeley: Counterpoint, 2011).

T. Wise, *Dear White America: Letter to a New Minority* (San Francisco: City Lights Books, 2012).

G. Yancy, *Backlash: What Happens When We Honestly Talk about Racism in America* (Lanham: Rowman and Littlefield, 2018).

Chapter 6. Intersectionality and 'implicit' or 'unconscious' bias

A. Brah and A. Phoenix, 'Ain't I a woman? Revisiting intersectionality', *Journal of International Women's Studies* 5 (3) (2004): 75–86.

N. Yuval Davis, *The Politics of Belonging: Intersectional Contestations* (London: Sage, 2011).

Chapter 7. The rise of right-wing national populism and the future of racism

A. Abramowitz, *The Great Alignment: Race, Party Transformation, and the Rise of Donald Trump* (New Haven: Yale University Press, 2018).

K. Cramer, *The Politics of Resentment: Rural Consciousness in Wisconsin* (Chicago: University of Chicago Press, 2016).

E. Dionne, Jr, N. Ornstein, and T. Mann, *One Nation After Trump* (New York: St. Martin's Press, 2017).

M. Hetherington and J. Weiler, *Authoritarianism and Polarization in American Politics* (Cambridge: Cambridge University Press, 2009).

P. Kristivo, *The Trump Phenomenon: How the Politics of Populism Won in 2016* (Bingley: Emerald Publishing, 2017).

C. Mudde (ed.), *The Populist Radical Right: A Reader* (Abingdon: Routledge, 2017).

W. Outhwaite, *Brexit: Sociological Responses* (London: Anthem Press, 2017).

R. Wodak, M. Khosravinik, and B. Mral (eds), *Right-Wing Populism in Europe: Politics and Discourse* (London: Bloomsbury, 2013).

Publisher's acknowledgements

We are grateful for permission to include the following copyright material in this book.

Extract from '"It amazes me that more isn't done to tackle it": readers on bias in Britain', *The Guardian*, 8 December 2018, Guardian News & Media.

The publisher and author have made every effort to trace and contact all copyright holders before publication. If notified, the publisher will be pleased to rectify any errors or omissions at the earliest opportunity.

Index

For the benefit of digital users, indexed terms that span two pages (e.g., 52–53) may, on occasion, appear on only one of those pages.

Racism

Index

U

Index